Men on the Bag

Men on the Bag
The Caddies of Augusta National

Ward Clayton

SPORTS MEDIA GROUP

Sports Media Group
an imprint of Ann Arbor Media Group
2500 S. State Street
Ann Arbor, Michigan 48104

Library of Congress Cataloging in Publication data on file.

08 07 06 05 04   1 2 3 4 5

Printed and bound at Edwards Brothers, Inc., Ann Arbor,
Michigan, U.S.A.

ISBN 1-58726-002-6

To my favorite foursome:
Mom, *Elizabeth,* Monica, *and* Will

Contents

Prologue

My favorite caddie story takes place on the fifteenth fairway at the Augusta National Golf Club, the same place where Stovepipe and Gene Sarazen contrived a miracle in 1935 and where numerous Masters have been won or lost coming down the stretch on Sunday. There are no famous names in this story, just an unknown Augusta National caddie handing out some basic advice one day to an unnamed player during a casual round of golf.

Faced with a shot of just under 200 yards to the green on the downhill par-5 hole, the player was torn about which club to use. He was in a quandary, complicating his next shot. Hit the easy 4-iron or the hard 5-iron, he asked?

Finally, the caddie blankly looked at the player and answered.

"It's the solid ball that'll carry," he said.

I don't know the result of the player's shot, but that piece of advice tells the story of Augusta National caddies: Simple, to the point. Just strike the ball solidly and the club choice won't matter as much.

As I researched material for this book, I kept coming back to this story and to my youth in Durham, North Carolina. A summer staple in the Bull City, the *Herald-Sun* Golf Classic is a week-long match-play tournament that originated before World War II and draws some of the top amateurs in the area and quite a few hacks that simply enjoy the camaraderie and head-to-head competition. Previous winners and medalists included future PGA Tour winners Skip Alexander, Mike Souchak, Jim Ferree, and Leonard Thompson. For those who grew up in Durham, the tournament had a Masters feel because it drew an unusually large gallery of friends, family, and the golf community, mainly because the newspaper treated the tournament with widespread coverage that was usually reserved for such revered events as Duke or North Carolina basketball. While learning to play the game as a preteen, I would walk the six blocks to Hillandale Golf Course and work as a forecaddie at the tournament, spotting tee shots on the par-4 twelfth hole for players such as Elbert Thorpe, the oldest brother of PGA Tour and Champions Tour player Jim Thorpe, and other local amateurs. Years later, as a participant, I learned the value of teamwork on the golf course. Young kids would volunteer to caddie for parents, siblings, or friends just so they could be in the mix and experience the competition. When players were eliminated from match play, it was not unusual to see sidelined golfers pick up the bag of a friend or relative and coax them on to victory. If they could not play, caddying was as close to the competitive fire as they could get. Caddying friends would brag to players that they could not win without the assistance.

I was fortunate enough to experience this on a higher level at Augusta National in 1986, the day after Jack Nicklaus won his sixth green jacket, as a part of the national media's one shot at walking the fairways. I was a young sports writer for the *Durham* (N.C.) *Morning Herald* when I rose at 5:30 A.M. on the Saturday of that tournament to get in line outside the media center for the privilege of signing up for Monday play. In those days, a first-come, first-serve sheet was posted on the front door of the old Quonset hut media center at 8:15 A.M. sharp. Much to my despair, I ended up as the first alternate, only to jump out of my seat in the media center twenty-four hours later when I was informed that someone was bumped because he had played on the Monday after the Masters a few years before.

The experience of playing the golf course was shared with a young Augusta National caddie, David Chestnut, who swore that he had looped for Nicklaus in a couple of practice rounds the week before the tournament when the oldest Nicklaus son, Jack II, had yet to arrive for caddying duties. David redirected my putts on the tricky putting surfaces, was dead-on with his club selection, and kept me smiling with idle conversation about everything under the sun except golf.

"Play it here," he pointed to a spot on the fifth green as I eyed a rare birdie chance.

"You're kidding me?" I said from a crouch behind the ball, shaking my head while reading the twenty-five-foot putt. I figured that the putt would start left of the hole and break back.

"This is it ... Trust me," David said.

His line guided me at least ten feet to the right of the back pin position. I followed his lead, at first uneasily because my back was nearly turned to the hole, and made a difficult two-putt par.

From tee to green, we talked about Michael Jordan's new NBA career, Augusta's own Godfather of Soul, James Brown, and where the best barbecue is served in Augusta. Golf strategy was a topic reserved for when we arrived for the next shot. I would estimate that seventy-five percent of my conversation that day was with David instead of my two playing companions.

The camaraderie eased the usual tension of playing golf on such hallowed ground. Simply having a caddie made the day considerably more enjoyable.

But I was also saddened during the preparation of this book. I learned that many of these men who became fixtures at Augusta National had lived the hard life and not benefited from their fame.

Augusta National caddies were not the most sophisticated lot in the world in their heyday. Many were uneducated and poor, searching for any job they could find to make a buck. A few had bad hygiene, especially poor dental work. They had no alternative but to loop at either Augusta Country Club (simply called "the country club") or "the National." Many ruined their caddie association with top players, blew their funds by making unwise gambles in life, and wasted their lives away in a bottle.

Some were not even the best at clubbing players or reading greens. Those rare birds, such as "Pappy" Stokes or Carl Jackson, who knew the course just by sight, go down in history as the great students of this storied course, keeping to themselves the "secrets" in reading the greens and figuring the swirling winds. Arnold Palmer and Jack Nicklaus seldom relied on the advice of "Iron Man" Avery or Willie Peterson in choosing clubs or reading putts. But to a fault, these caddies knew how to get a player around the golf course in the least number of strokes by passing along their knowledge of the course's subtleties or knowing when to push the player's buttons. Who can forget the 1960 Masters when "Iron Man" inspired Arnie with his famous comment late on Sunday, "Are we chokin'?"

"Golf's not my game," Matthew "Shorty Mac" Palmer once said of his playing ability. "Knowing about golf is my game."

"You can't just read these greens," Marion Herrington said. "You've got to remember them."

Reading yardages and putts was not the limit for these men.

"You had to know the elements," Jariah Beard says. "It was more than telling somebody they had 130 yards to the pin. Nobody can be that exact. You had to know the conditions and get the feel of the player, see how he was feeling at that time. He might be pumped up a little. He might be hitting the ball solid, he might not be. It's not just how far it is to the hole or how far the putt breaks."

Their standing as the game's most famous and respected caddie corps carries forward simply because they were a cast of characters who added a dimension to the Masters that no other golf tournament had. The U.S. Open, British Open, and PGA Championship, the game's other professional majors, all move from site to site annually. Until the caddie ranks were opened, these tournaments did not have a consistent cast of loopers that the golf public and top players could latch on to every spring like the Masters. Many times, kids at the local clubs reserved for the U.S. Open or PGA were forced into action, purely as someone to carry the bag around for eighteen holes. The British Open offered caddies, but they were not always attached to the host club. But the Masters was different. Where else could you see Willie Peterson every year whipping his towel toward a Nicklaus putt or Gary Player and Eddie McCoy walking arm-in-arm up to the eighteenth green in 1978?

Or look at Edward White, a former caddie who now helps organize the caddie ranks and golf carts at Augusta National. He walks around with a nickel lodged in his ear to this day. Why?

"I'm down to my last nickel," he says with a sheepish grin as you laugh out loud despite the corny punch line.

Or listen to the late Leon McCladdie. The caddie for two-time Masters champion Tom Watson had the opportunity in 1979 to caddie for longtime *Atlanta Journal-Constitution* columnist Furman Bisher. Bisher, a left-hander with a 14 handicap, was playing a casual round at Augusta National and kept noticing the grimace on McCladdie's face, especially when Furman hooked his tee shot near the thirteenth tee on the par-3 twelfth hole.

"Well, Tom Weiskopf took a 13 here," Furman told McCladdie.

"You ain't through yet," McCladdie shot back.

That is why the World Golf Hall of Fame in St. Augustine, Florida, has a display about caddies with a photo of the Augusta National caddies and a voice-over by former longtime caddie master Freddie Bennett.

They were and remain a proud group of men, still disturbed by the sudden change in policy in 1983 that allowed "outside" caddies to tote on their home turf. For every player who has stated he did not rely on the caddie's input, that same caddie will respond that there were at least five key moments in the round when the player heeded his advice. Name a Masters champion before 1983, and I will bet his caddie did something that week that inspired his victory, whether it involved strategy or by simply being a part of the team.

The caddie comes closer than anyone in any sport to feeling the pulse of athletic competition on the highest level. Coaches, referees, and umpires are on the same playing surface in other sports, but they are mere observers and do not consult with the player just as a key play is being executed.

They do not stand behind the quarterback while he reads the defensive alignment and awaits the snap in football. They cannot peer in at the catcher just as the pitcher goes into his motion against the power hitter. They are not in a position to hand the basketball to the forward just before he prepares for a last-second free throw against the backdrop of a hostile crowd. Imagine standing on the twelfth tee at Augusta National on a Sunday afternoon, in the heat of the battle, with the CBS cameras focused in from the stand to the right and front of the tee. The Amen Corner crowd covers the hillside and grandstands behind the par-3 tee and spreads toward the eleventh and thirteenth fairways, standing on tiptoes to get a glimpse. A hush comes over the gallery, and it is quiet enough to hear

Sam Snead (*right*) and his caddie O'Bryant Williams had an unusual and humorous relationship. Snead once told Williams not to talk to him during a round, which Williams lived up to despite Snead's urging for some assistance during a round. (© *Augusta Chronicle*)

the birds sing and the wind rushing through the tall pine trees. The green and white scoreboard on the opposite side of the eleventh green tells the story. There you stand, talking with a player about the swirling winds, the exact yardage, and what club to choose. One wrong move and the green jacket drowns in Rae's Creek.

I am reminded of Johnny Miller and Mark Eubanks in this instance. "Banks" was such a worrier on the course while caddying for Miller that Johnny prohibited him from touching the grips of his clubs in fear that Mark's profuse sweating would make his grips slippery. Still, Miller found comfort in his caddie's nervous demeanor, perhaps because he realized he could not possibly be as torn up about a golf tournament as Eubanks.

Or take the case of Sam Snead and O'Bryant Williams, the caddie in his 1949, 1952, and 1954 Masters victories. Slammin' Sammy wanted absolutely no input on club selection from his caddie and told him that bluntly beforehand one year. But one round they came to the par-3 sixth tee and the wind was blowing in a different direction than normal. Sam was perplexed, so he asked O'Bryant if he remembered which way the wind was blowing the previous day, even reassuring him that there would not be any ramifications for his advice.

"I ain't talking, I ain't talking," O'Bryant said over and over as he shook his head. "I know what you're trying to do and you ain't gonna give me hell."

O'Bryant never told Sam which way the wind was blowing. O'Bryant was living up to his word.

O'Bryant's enthusiasm was undaunted, however. In the classic eighteen-hole play-off with Ben Hogan in 1954, Snead trailed by one entering the par-5 thirteenth. He hit the green in two and had a makeable eagle putt. As the putt approached the hole, O'Bryant started screaming, "Get in! Get in," and started waving his hand at the ball. The putt missed, Snead tapped in for birdie and was even with five holes to play on the way to a one-stroke victory, his final Masters title.

"O'Bryant, if you had hit that ball with your hand I would

have buried you right in that there green," Snead told *Golf Digest* in 1983.

Snead's penchant for humor was never lost on his association with his caddie. The story goes that O'Bryant fathered a large family, numbering as many as fourteen children. Every year, Snead would bet twenty dollars that O'Bryant could not name all of his children. O'Bryant never could, which gave Snead a big laugh, but O'Bryant was always paid that twenty dollars.

Loyalty is always evident among Augusta National caddies. When Lee Elder became the first black man to play in the Masters in 1975, Billy "Baldy" Ricks took the bus from his home in California to his native Augusta just to be there. Ricks, afraid of flying, said the bus stopped in Phoenix and on came a tiny, elderly black lady, who happened to be Elder's godmother, and she rode all the way to Augusta beside him. It was the only time the Augusta National caddie ever used a ticket to attend the tournament, one he acquired from an Augusta National member who was his age and a longtime friend.

When Ron Townsend became the first black member of the club in 1991, the caddies made a point to search him out and give him a simple handshake. When Greg Puga, a Hispanic caddie at Bel-Air Country Club in Los Angeles, made the 2001 Masters as the U.S. Public Links champion, he hired Joe Collins. The veteran Augusta National caddie called it one of his proudest moments, despite Puga missing the cut, and said it was almost as good as getting the bag of a potential Masters champion.

Acknowledgments

I could not go through this entryway to the story of the Augusta National caddies without mentioning some people who lent me a hand.

The *Augusta Chronicle*, where I worked as sports editor from 1991 to 2000, was extremely helpful in the research on photographs and old stories.

Of particular note is sports writer David Westin, who has probably written more words about Augusta National and the Masters than anyone else in the world during his twenty-five-plus years at the *Chronicle*. David goes by the nickname "Ghost," perhaps because he moonlighted as a caddie at Augusta National in the late 1980s. But more likely, David earned his nickname because of his quiet demeanor. The *Chronicle* had a policy that disallowed employees to hold second jobs, but David wanted to caddie and worked during the day at the National when time permitted. One day, David found himself in the same foursome as Billy Morris, an Augusta National member and the newspaper's longtime owner and publisher. Remembering the no-moonlighting rule, David tried to lie low, pulling his green caddie cap down over his eyes and planning to stay on the opposite sides of fairways and greens from Mr. Morris as often as possible. However, Mr. Morris spotted him from the outset and strolled over with a smile on his face.

"You know, David, it's very industrious of you to be out here caddying," Mr. Morris said, surprising David.

In addition, I am indebted to Rob Carr, the newspaper's director of photography. Rob was understanding about my frequent requests for photos of old and current caddies. Dennis Sodomka, the longtime executive editor of the *Chronicle*, also lent his support for this project when I worked for him in Augusta and beyond. The newspaper's archived Web site, augustaarchives.com, is also quite an innovation in on-line research, allowing viewers to step back in time to the early 1800s without actually sitting in front of a microfilm machine.

Other thanks go to good friends Donna and Stan Byrdy, with Stan being a former sportscaster in Augusta and a current successful author of golf history in Augusta and neighboring Aiken, South Carolina; Glenn Greenspan, who serves as Director of Communications at Augusta National; Kathleen Beasley, who helps look after Pappy along with his sisters and brother; the Willie Peterson family (Vanessa and brother Russell); Will Kennedy, my former associate and boss in Augusta; and the folks at the Ann Arbor Media Group for encouraging the completion of this book.

Also, love goes out to Elizabeth, my wife, and our cherished children, Monica and Will, who put up with my late nights and hour upon hour of research and writing to complete a project that I had only dreamed about previously. That same love goes to in-laws Bill, Monica, and John Patterson, who share my enthusiasm for all sports. To my parents, Edith and the late Elmo Clayton, I cannot express enough gratitude for their encouragement to explore writing as a career.

Finally, and most of all, thanks go to the Augusta National caddies who told the tales of their cohorts. Carl Jackson is a rock of a man who has persisted during his life and is dedicated to his family, foremost. Tall and quiet, I am sure he was very easy for Ben Crenshaw to lean on in the challenging times that they have spent on and off the course. Jariah Beard has a passion for golf and caddying, creating great memories. Also, thanks to Joe Collins, Pappy Stokes, Bennie Hatcher, Buck Moore, Louis Laurence, Tommy Bennett, Billy Ricks, Marion Herrington, Robert Bass, and anyone who has ever carried a golf bag at Augusta National.

All you have to do is sit for a few minutes with some of these former caddies and you will be hooked. Their deep passion for the sport and a competitive fire second to none are evident from the outset. They know more than just the golf games of Jones and Hogan and Snead and Nicklaus and Palmer and Woods. They can recite the mannerisms and the personality traits that created an ability to win the Masters.

Playing Augusta National would be a dream day for any golf fan. Having a caddie with such great knowledge and instinct increases the joy immeasurably.

Introduction

Begin with the crisp, bright white jumpsuit. Top it with a green baseball cap inscribed with the cursive "Caddie." Ground it with the white Foot-Joy tennis shoes, trimmed in green. This is the uniform of the world's most famous caddie corps.

Add the mind of a scout, scanning the landscape to find any clues on how to tame the swirling winds of Amen Corner or read the hidden breaks in the most deceptive greens on earth. Include the timing of a comedian, ready to break the tension of Sunday's back nine at the Masters Tournament with the simplest statement or gestures. And do not forget the heart of a daredevil, prepared to challenge his boss on a decision, any time or anywhere.

A caddie's checklist of duties is physically and mentally taxing. One week of work at the Augusta National Golf Club during the Masters consists of more than thirty walking miles (four-plus miles per eighteen-hole round) up and down the extremely rolling terrain to scout tee and pin placements before tournament rounds begin and during practice rounds and in tournament play. On most days of Masters Week, the caddie may arrive at dawn and not leave the grounds until dusk more than twelve hours later after escorting his player to the practice range, the putting green, the course, and back to the practice areas again to close the day. Add in the unpredictable weather of early April in Augusta, which could range from the chilly 40s to wet conditions to high humidity with temperatures in the 80s. These factors contribute to the difficult chore of carrying a fifty-pound golf bag packed with clubs, balls, rain gear, minor medical supplies, and light snacks. The caddie must also keep his player's clubs clean and dry, check that his fourteen-club limit is met just before tee-off, stay attentive to each player's scoring in his group and the overall standings on the scoreboards, and also serve as a one-man gallery marshal when his player addresses the ball. Include the knowledge of standing in the proper place so as not to distract any players, keeping up with the pace of play and expertly tending flags, replacing divots, and raking bunkers. And, most importantly, the caddie must serve as a psychologist, trying to figure the mood and level of play for his player on that day. When the time comes, what should he say and how forcefully? Will the player be able to hit the required shot under the gun to a dangerous pin position, based on his warm-up session that morning and his play over the previous holes that day?

These are the characteristics that made up what has universally been acclaimed as the greatest band of men to ever carry a golf bag, the caddies at the Augusta National Golf Club. They were recognized as the most astute surveyors of the most difficult greens that the game had to offer. They were also the confidants to the game's greatest players. They were Tonto to the Lone Ranger, Barney to Andy, Robin to Batman, Keith Richards to Mick Jagger.

These caddies and their stories through the years have formed just as much a fixture of the Masters Tournament and Augusta National as the azaleas, slick greens, green jacket, and pimento cheese sandwiches.

The caddies who have toted golf bags at Augusta National over the years have become famous and colorful seconds to those who played on golf's hallowed ground and won its most famous tournament. Just remember:

- Gene Sarazen and Stovepipe, with his tall, silk hat
- Ben Hogan and Pappy, who was born on the grounds before Augusta National was even a dream
- President Eisenhower and musically inclined Cemetery

- Arnold Palmer and the stoic Iron Man
- Jack Nicklaus and his excitable lucky charm Willie Peterson
- Ben Crenshaw and the quiet, perceptive Carl Jackson

Many Masters participants or Augusta National members and their guests have been coached and humored by a caddie who could sleepwalk the 365 acres at the corner of Washington and Berckmans roads, particularly the unforeseen breaks on the famous greens. Who else can claim to know more about the inner workings as a player enters the psychological maze of the back nine at Augusta National on a Sunday afternoon in early April?

But things are different now. The spotlight long ago faded here. Iron Man and Willie Peterson, on the bag of a combined ten Masters victories, are dead, as are many of the famously named caddies of yesteryear. Pappy approaches age eighty-four, his vision growing worse and worse and his mobility lessening, but his get up and go still harkens back sixty years. Carl Jackson is the last vestige, hanging on with longtime friend Crenshaw.

More than twenty years ago, the rule forcing participants to use only Augusta National caddies in the Masters was absolved. Since 1983, the home club's contribution has continually dwindled. Most players bring their regular PGA Tour or European Tour caddies, marquee names like Fluff, Fanny, Bones, and Stevie. The wide-eyed amateurs often bring friends, instructors, or relatives to share the once-in-a-lifetime experience of being the only "outsider" allowed inside the ropes with the contestant. Many a senior player whose Masters win is lost in the years, unable to compete for the title or even make the cut any longer, will grant a special wish to an associate to tote the bag in the sunset of a career.

So, the Augusta National caddies wait from their home base in the caddie shack that sits behind a tall stand of shrubbery to the right of the first fairway. Maybe a contender will visit Augusta National in the weeks preceding the tournament on a fact-finding mission and pick up a National caddie. Maybe, just maybe, that brief encounter will convince the player that it could be a good idea to gain some local knowledge in the tournament itself. They just hope to grab a bone now and then, praying that a veteran player, hotshot amateur, or emergency pickup of a decent player can lead to a big weekend paycheck. Better yet, the weeks outside of the Masters—regular member play—are considered far more valuable now. When an Augusta National caddie gets a bag for the Masters and then misses the cut, the weeks following are a final chance for a big payday. Who knows? You might latch on to the occasional celebrity such as Michael Jordan or former President George Bush. Even a well-heeled member, such as a Bill Gates or Warren Buffet, would make for a memorable payday and possibly a regular association for years.

"It doesn't feel too good," says Joe Collins, a thirty-two-year veteran who claims a third with Jim Jamieson in 1973 as his best finish. "But I'm not bitter; it's just something that happens."

Others do not fade away quite as easily. Bennie Hatcher started caddying at Augusta National in 1963, worked for Arnold Palmer (following Iron Man) from 1969 to 1977, and later for Lanny Wadkins. His ire is aimed at the fact that the basic caddying code that made Augusta National caddies the game's benchmark is all but forgotten.

"As the years have progressed, a new generation of people has been coming on," Hatcher says. "We used to go out there and try to out-caddie each other, bet three dollars that your man could beat their man. And you worked it hard. You'd learn and try to feed off each other.

"Now, many people who caddie here come around just interested in making money. They don't give a damn whether they learn or not. They just say, 'How much does he pay? I want to go with him.'"

Freddie Bennett, the forty-plus years caddie master at Augusta National, retired in 2000 and on his way out the door swore he would never step foot back on the grounds, except for maybe an occasional tournament visit. Bennett was a former caddie who rose in rank to become responsible for creating many a winning Masters pair, a man with the sense to help find suitable personalities such as a Jariah Beard for Masters rookie Fuzzy Zoeller, the winner in 1979, or Peterson with Nicklaus. He is a member of the Professional Caddies Association Hall of Fame and was the first recipient of the Reynolds Caddie Medal, an annual award given by Augusta National member Dr. John Reynolds, an Augusta native, in memory of his parents and in honor of all caddies in the state of Georgia.

For his four years before retirement, Bennett was simply a figurehead, titled Director of Outside Operations, perched on a stool in the bag room that sits on the end of the clubhouse, just to the right of the first tee. Augusta National opted to modernize its caddie system and Bennett got lost in the shuffle.

Caddie Master Enterprises, a Pinehurst, North Carolina, company that trains and provides caddies for some of the nation's most prestigious golf courses, including Pinehurst Resort, Blackwolf Run, and Sea Island, Georgia, was hired in October 1996 to oversee Augusta National's caddie corps. Tom Van Dorn, a white man, was brought in to serve as the caddie master and work with a crew of more than 100 men, a mix of Augusta National veterans and newcomers from all reaches of the country, during the club's October–May season. Caddies today at Augusta National fit a varied range. There are the college-age kids looking for a once-in-a-lifetime opportunity to caddie at Augusta National. There are the promising young players looking for a few bucks to carry them on to mini-tours and the dream of one day playing the PGA Tour. Then there are the devoted caddies, such as Augusta's own Louis Laurence, who want to be involved in the game and make a living year-round. Finally, there are the grizzled veterans of Augusta National who hang on mainly because they need the money and do not have another occupation that fits their accustomed lifestyle.

No doubt, the new caddie system is good business, with better organization, more training up front, a refined method of picking caddies for everyday play, and more equal benefits, including unemployment during the off-season, if necessary. But just like what occurred more than twenty years ago, much of the personality in being an Augusta National caddie has been diminished. The outgoing, individual caddies with distinct characteristics are not evident anymore.

By 1997, not a single regular Augusta National caddie worked the tournament. Only Jackson with Crenshaw and Brian Poole, with amateur "Spider" Miller, made the Augusta National connection. Ironically, Poole, a white man who grew up in Augusta, would later become a Caddie Master Enterprises caddie master during the 1999 U.S. Open at Pinehurst No. 2.

The number of Masters caddies with Augusta National ties has never reached double figures in succeeding years. In 2001, there was a sudden rush of National caddies, led by Jackson and including Robert Bass with amateur Jeff Quinney, Collins with amateur Greg Puga, Hatcher with amateur Milo Ilonen, Marion Herrington with amateur James Driscoll, Freddie Robertson with former Masters champion Tommy Aaron, and Ronald Whitfield with two-time Masters champion Seve Ballesteros. Bass even did double time that week, working as a dishwasher at the ultra-busy Outback Steakhouse on Washington Road until late at night and caddying during the day.

The introduction of "outsiders" to the caddie equation, both the Tour caddies and the caddie management group, distanced Augusta National and the Masters even further from Augusta's black community, which makes up more than fifty percent of home base Richmond County's population. When Augusta National had its all-black caddie corps and an all-white field (prior to Lee Elder's participation in 1975), there was a perception of racial division nationally and internationally. The club was criticized for its closed-door policy and decidedly private way of dealing with issues. However, the majority of the caddies did not consider their racial makeup a put down; it was an opportunity.

They carried the bags at the National because they could unify to prove their worth as a group of accomplished men who plied a rare trade. They wanted to be known as the best their profession could offer, a creed very much consistent with Augusta National's motto across the board, whether it be an

Caddie Jariah Beard enjoys a victory cigar in the caddie shack after Fuzzy Zoeller's 1979 Masters victory. Beard still has Zoeller's Power Bilt golf bag *(left)* stored in the attic of his Augusta home. (© *Augusta Chronicle*)

immaculate golf course and surrounding landscape or the precise manner in which club members and employees carried themselves. They learned the golf course as best as humanly possible and dressed impeccably in the bright white, wrinkle-free jumpsuits. Many of the caddies came from the Sand Hill section of Augusta, up on the hill above Augusta Country Club and within easy walking distance of both courses. They learned the caddie game as youngsters at Augusta Country Club, went on to Augusta National and, hopefully, to one day as the caddie for a winning Masters champion.

"We did it because we had a long-standing pride in what we did," says former Augusta National caddie Jariah Beard, Fuzzy Zoeller's caddie in 1979. "You don't know how much money that took out of the black community. It devastated a lot of guys because they depended on that money to hold them over from when the course closed in May for the summer until it opened again the next October. That just wore a lot of the guys out."

In many ways, the black community in Augusta had more to celebrate in those days than it does today, even with the emergence of Tiger Woods.

Tiger is a point of pride in that he reached the pinnacle of what was once an all-white sport and has undoubtedly brought more people to the game who previously had no interest in playing golf, much less watching the sport. The First Tee, a national program focused on offering access to golf for those who previously had not received the opportunity, sprang up. Augusta has a beautiful small course and clubhouse located on Damascus Road, just over one block from Forest Hills Golf Club, on the former site of low-rent apartments. Beard is one of many community members who have recently tried to infuse more interest and involvement from within the young black community of inner-city Augusta.

The black community's involvement with the Masters pales in comparison to what it used to be. The Monday after the Masters always began a huge week of celebration in Augusta's black community for years and years. In the 1950s, a number of nationally recognized celebrities began to emerge from

Augusta's black community, including the "Godfather of Soul," James Brown, and opera superstar Jessye Norman. Their notoriety added to the luster of this group. All of the Augusta National employees, including the caddies, waiters, ground maintenance, and other jobs, received their paychecks on the Monday after the Masters. Cab drivers, hotel workers, and other employees around the periphery of the tournament also welcomed the week after when they could relax. It was a time to celebrate their contribution to Augusta's most visible event. Usually at the center of the celebration was the winning caddie, first because he had become famous the previous Sunday and he had garnered the largest paycheck.

"You'd have set parties—at the American Legion, at the Elks Club," Beard remembers. "We had a good time. There would be bands, disc jockeys, and big crowds. Black businesses thrived that week too because it was a time for everybody to celebrate. When less and less caddies started to work the tournament and less of us came from Augusta it was absolutely all gone."

Nevertheless, the memories still exist as if it was yesterday. And they are good ones.

"There ain't many of us left anymore," Beard says. "A lot of those guys who were coming along in the early 1980s found something else to do. Our stories get us by now."

The Caddies

Four Augusta National caddies watch tee shots from their positions on the fairway during the 1974 Masters Tournament. (Photograph by Danny Rogers, © *Augusta Chronicle*)

The Nicknames:
From Baldy to Waynesboro

Remember when you were a kid and your group of friends hung out at school, on the playground, in the back yard, at the mall, just about everywhere? Everybody had to have a nickname to portray the closeness of the group. David or Charles or Steve just would not do. Last names were also too formal. If somebody called you by your given name, they were way out of touch.

The tough, athletic kid was labeled "Concrete." The heavyset kid who craved fried chicken from a certain fast-food chicken establishment was called "Chicken Hut," or "Hut" for short. Another went by a shortened version of his father's unusual name, "'Mo." The new kid in the neighborhood was dubbed "New Kid."

That is how caddies developed their colorful nicknames. Hours in the caddie shack or on the course led to these names. Only their names catch on for life, not just until high school graduation. Caddies live by their nicknames instead of their given names. Mike Cowan? No, it's "Fluff." Willie Perteet? That's got to be "Cemetery."

This tradition is based on the first caddies in the game. History lessons say that caddies first were heard about in the 1500s when Mary, Queen of Scots, went to France as a young girl. The King of France had the first golf course outside of

Scotland built for her. The king hired cadets from a military school to guard Mary as she played golf. When Mary returned to Scotland from France at age eighteen, she brought a number of the uniformed lads back with her. One of their duties back home in Scotland was to follow Mary around the links and carry her clubs. In French, cadet is pronounced "ca-day." Cadets soon became "caddies," simply because of the Scottish pronunciation.

One of the earliest written references to caddies appears in the record of Andrew Dixon, a golf ball maker in the early eighteenth century who lived near Edinburgh, Scotland, and worked for Mary's grandson, the Duke of York (future King James II).

The famous Scottish links courses had the first caddies of renown, bearing nicknames such as Big, Fiery, Ol' Da, Skipper, Poot, and Pawkey. By the 1880s, when golf was first played in the United States, caddies became evident here also. World Golf Hall of Famers such as Francis Quimet, Gene Sarazen, Byron Nelson, and Ben Hogan all got their starts in golf by serving as young caddies early in the twentieth century.

The Augusta National caddies have developed a wide assortment of caddie nicknames, most in relation to a physical characteristic or a particular incident that affected their lives. These colorful monikers offer a glimpse into who the caddies really were.

For example, Nathaniel "Iron Man" Avery earned his nickname because he survived some sort of physically harmful experience, such as a knife fight or firecracker explosion, with little damage.

Sarazen's Masters caddie, Stovepipe, earned his simply because he wore a tall, silk, black hat that resembled a stovepipe.

Many of the Augusta National caddies are known by only these titles. There is seldom a record of Stovepipe's given name, but research reveals that his given name was the unusual Thor Nordwall.

Willie "Tassall" Mason and "Big Henry" Avery, who served as successive caddie masters at Augusta Country Club, labeled many of the caddies with nicknames when they were just starting to caddie. Augusta Country Club was the place where teenage caddies first went to work before "going across the creek" to Augusta National. Saturday mornings were reserved for caddie lessons for school-age caddies, with Mason showing the youngsters the ropes and even giving playing lessons and conducting informal tournaments on the practice facility at Augusta Country Club.

"Big Henry would yell from the caddie house over there to get some caddies to work," Carl Jackson remembers of his first experiences at the country club. "We'd be standing in a field across from the country club waiting for a bag. If (Henry) didn't know your name, he would call you by what you looked like or who you were related to. My big brother (Austin) was 'Tweety.' (Henry) didn't know my name, so he just called me 'Little Tweet.'"

John Henry Williams, nicknamed "Eleven," and his successor Freddie Bennett as caddie master at Augusta National handed down other nicknames when caddies "graduated" to Augusta National.

The caddies even gave nicknames to the golfers. Iron Man often referred to his longtime player Arnold Palmer as simply "Par." Gary Player earned the nickname "The Aferkin" around the caddie shack because of his South African heritage. Willie Peterson simply called Jack Nicklaus, "Mr. Jack."

Sidney Matthew, the Bobby Jones' historian, caddied for PGA Tour pro Kenny Knox, a friend, in the 1991 Masters. Matthew was asked where he was from and his occupation during a pre-tournament visit to the caddie shack. When he told the surrounding caddies that he was an attorney in Tallahassee, Florida, Matthew was labeled with the nickname, "The Judge."

"By the end of the week I was asked by every caddie there about how to handle a divorce, a ticket, any legal action," Matthew said. "They just said, 'Hey, Judge, I got this problem...' "

The golf course earned its own nicknames, also. The big hill on the par-5 eighth hole climbs nearly 70 feet from the tee shot landing area to just more than 100 yards short of the green. The caddies have labeled it "Big Bertha," because of the difficult walk and the two noteworthy moguls that sit on the top of the hill, reminding the caddies of a woman's shapely figure.

Following are some of the more colorful Augusta National caddie nicknames, with a short explanation where available. Many of the nicknames are obvious.

Pappy: Willie Stokes. The five-time winner as a Masters caddie was given the nickname by his family when he was small because of his slow, pensive movement and attitude, like an old man.

Cemetery or Dead Man: Willie Perteet. Ike's caddie survived a knife attack from a dumped girlfriend and her friends. He was left for dead in the hospital morgue before reviving. Therefore the nickname, which President Eisenhower altered from Dead Man to Cemetery.

Burnt Biscuits: Tommy Bennett. Tiger Woods' first Masters caddie burned his legs when he turned over a pot of boiling water while trying to escape through a window after stealing some fresh biscuits that were cooling on his grandmother's wood-burning stove.

Pete: Willie Peterson. Nicklaus' caddie simply had a shortened version of his last name. Also called Brother or 'Bro.

Skillet: Carl Jackson. Ben Crenshaw's caddie was given the name when he was a young baseball player in Augusta "because I pitched and couldn't break an egg. I just threw junk." Also called Little Tweet (after his older brother) or Booger because he had a habit as a youngster of picking his nose.

Daybreak: Bennie Hatcher. No, Arnold Palmer's Masters caddie through most of the 1970s did not stay up all night partying and show up at the course just in time to caddie as the nickname would infer. "I never showed up late. I was always at the course early in the morning. Before sun up. That's where that came from," says Hatcher, who succeeded Iron Man on Palmer's bag.

Waynesboro: Marion Herrington. The caddie for winner Seve Ballesteros in 1980 was born in Waynesboro, Georgia, about thirty minutes south of Augusta. He now serves as the caddie master at Sage Valley Golf Club, a new, exclusive private club across the Savannah River in Graniteville, South Carolina. A handful of former Augusta National caddies have also landed at the club.

Edgar Allen Poe. No nickname, but the given name of an old Augusta National caddie. "Poe?" an Augusta National guest once asked about his caddie's name when introduced. "Like the poet, Edgar Allan Poe?" "That's me," the caddie shot back. "How did you know?"

Po Baby: Ron Whitfield. Given to him because he was always complaining, possibly also because he lacked money. When Whitfield picked up Ballesteros' bag in 2000, he made sure to track down Seve at the end of the second round after the two-time champion missed the cut. "Got to go," he remarked to a group that he was talking with as he sprinted away. "I hear he don't pay if you don't find him after the round."

Shorty Mac: Matthew Palmer. Short in stature, but a great greens reader. He guided Billy Casper to his 1970 victory. It took six years before Casper finally listened to Palmer's advice on the greens. In an eighteen-hole play-off with Gene Littler, Casper took only twenty-seven putts, twelve on the front nine, and had nine one-putt greens. "I'm just hard-headed, I guess," Casper said about why he did not listen to Palmer earlier.

Skinny: Frank Ware. Tall, thin man who led George Archer to 1969 victory.

Eleven: John Henry Williams. Nickname for the Augusta National caddie master from 1945 to 1959. Earned nickname because he wore a No. 11 caddie badge before he became caddie master.

Big Boy: Jim Dent. One of the first black golfers to successfully compete on the PGA Tour and he has made a bigger name for himself on the Champions Tour over the last decade. Big Boy earned his nickname because of his size (six-feet-three, 225 pounds) and prodigious length off the tee. Dent once caddied for Bob Goalby in the Masters. He played high school football in the late 1950s at Augusta's all-black Laney

High School with future New York Jets Super Bowl fullback Emerson Boozer. On the PGA Tour, Dent had a high finish of second to Jack Nicklaus at the 1972 Walt Disney tournament and accumulated just over $500,000 in winnings from 1970 to 1988. He has won twelve times and earned more than $8.5 million in his fifteen-year career on the Champions Tour.

Beaver: Wallace Ware. Famous for once quitting on the twelfth hole while on the bag of a rude and demanding Englishman who was the guest of a member. The guest kept putting down Beaver and would not take his advice. Finally, Beaver had enough. "Mister, they pays me to carry your bag, not kiss your ass," he said as he dropped the startled guest's bag at Amen Corner and walked in. Beaver also once told a member whom he regularly caddied for and worked for off the course that he needed a loan: "Boss, I got lots of dust in my wallet."

Harrisburg: Johnny Garrett. Raised and lives in the Harrisburg section of Augusta. Harrisburg is one of the oldest caddies to continue working at Augusta National.

Iron Man: Nathaniel Avery. Arnie's caddie earned his nickname as a youngster because of his durability but folklore says that he survived an accident with a firecracker or an axe or knife attack.

Baldy: James "Billy" Ricks. Lacked hair. In the late 1940s, he thought original Augusta National pro Ed Dudley was praising his ability to quickly pick up balls on the driving range instead of talking about his receding hairline.

Little Earl: Jariah Beard. Fuzzy Zoeller's caddie in the 1979 victory earned this nickname because Earl was his father's name. Also called Bubba because that was another one of his father's nicknames.

Marble Eye: Frank Stokes (no relation to Pappy). He had large eyes. Marble Eye was on Goalby's bag in his controversial 1968 victory. Earned $2,500 from Goalby, for whom he caddied occasionally away from Augusta National. When Stokes, an Atlantan who was good friends with another Masters caddie, George "Fireball" Franklin, showed up for the next tournament after the Masters, he was sporting gaudy green alligator shoes and fancy new duds. "I'm not caddying this week, Bob," he said proudly.

Wheezy: Fred Searles. Not his given nickname but should have been. After winning with Byron Nelson in 1937 and 1942, Nelson had to find a new caddie soon after. Searles started wheezing on the practice tee before a round and his breathing got so bad he had to quit midway through the front nine. Turned out he had emphysema.

Hop: Fred Harrison. Raymond Floyd's caddie in his 1976 victory. Also called Hopalong because he walked with a limp since one leg was shorter than the other. He earned the nickname from an Athens, Georgia, attorney after Harrison was run over by a car as a child.

Bull: Charles I. Williams Jr. The longtime driving range supervisor at Augusta National. He was given his nickname because of his stocky build when he played inside linebacker in football at Laney High School. He has been responsible for handing out the practice balls on the range for decades and can usually be spotted under the large oak tree to the right of the teeing area. Also—in no disrespect to this Bull—a derogatory nickname for a caddie, according to Beard. The name suggested that a caddie was ignorant.

Stabber: A flattering term for a caddie, Beard says, because it means "you could pull clubs that went right to the heart of the green."

First Baseman: Cleveland Holmes. Played first base in baseball as a youth.

Snipes: Ernest Nipper. Gary Player's caddie for his first Masters victory in 1961. Also called Nip, but the Snipes moniker was more descriptive since he was labeled as a caddie who could read a golf course like a sniper with a rifle.

E.B.: Eddie McCoy. Player's caddie for his last two Masters victories was called by the initials of his first two names.

Mutt: Mutt Boyd. Ken Venturi's caddie. Mutt had a brother that everyone called Dude Boyd.

Fireball: George Franklin. Doug Ford's temperamental caddie in their 1957 victory who would disagree with Ford's strategy.

Cricket: Walter Pritchett. Crickett resembled a sheik with his towel headdress in Charles Coody's 1971 victory. Earned his nickname because of his tall, lanky build.

Hicky: Wayne Hawes.

Red: Tim Reid. Ruddy complexion and red hair.

Banks: Mark Eubanks. Johnny Miller's former caddie who was one of the authors of a manual on how to caddie at Augusta National. In the May 2002 issue of *Golf Digest*, Miller said he was saddened to hear that Eubanks had passed away. Come to find out, Eubanks was still alive and kicking, even though he was ill in the summer of 2003.

Pookie: James Harrison.

Cigarette: Robert Jones. Calvin Peete's occasional Tour and Masters caddie needed a nickname to differentiate from Bobby Jones, the cofounder of Augusta National. Obviously, he was a heavy smoker.

Round Head: Walter Newton. Had a round head.

Gardoolie: Guy Dooley. Two names were run together to form his nickname.

Shoo Poon: George Brooks.

Eight Ball: Clarence Harris. Earned the nickname because of his dark skin, like an eight ball in billiards. Pulled off a rare double in 1955 by carrying for winner Cary Middlecoff in the Masters and for Patty Berg in The Titleholders, the women's version of the Masters that was held at Augusta Country Club through the 1960s.

Long Distance: Given name unknown.

Pokie: Leepot Dent. Jim Dent's nephew.

Rat: James Gilbert. Earned nickname because he had short, pointed teeth, like a rat.

Cadillac: Given name unknown.

Lamb Chop: Given name unknown.

Bodiddly: Eugene Jones.

Cross-handed Henry: Henry Brown. Played golf cross-handed. He worked on two of the most controversial bags in Masters history. He worked for Roberto De Vicenzo in the Argentinian's 1968 Masters loss to Bob Goalby where De Vicenzo incorrectly signed his scorecard and failed to make a play-off with Goalby. In 1975, Brown worked for Lee Elder, the first black man to play in the Masters. He impressed Elder with his playing ability, as Elder invited him to play in an Elder-sponsored tournament in Virginia after the 1975 tournament. Beard contends that Brown may have been the best golfer ever among Augusta National caddies. "I played him one day and he beat me 5-up playing cross-handed right-handed," Beard recalled. "The next day he said he'd play me left-handed and he dusted me that way, too."

Eggy: Horace Avery. Eggy is the brother of Iron Man. Horace earned his nickname because he had a bump on his head that resembled a fried egg.

The First Caddie

William Bowman frequently swam in Rae's Creek as a teenager. He was not hunting golf balls. There was not even a golf course on the grounds at the time. The land at the corner of Washington and Berckmans Road was still called Fruitland Nurseries.

"We used to go swimming in that water," Bowman told the *Boston Globe* in 1990. "There were alligators in there. We'd sell the baby alligators to the hospital. They had an aquarium, and they'd put them in there and let the kids see them."

Bowman was resourceful enough to make a living in a couple of ways just before and after Augusta National was first built and the Masters Tournament—then called the Augusta National Invitation Tournament—debuted. For three years, he secretly ran a still in the woods where the course would be built. In the days of Prohibition, Bowman sold half-pints of moonshine for twenty-five cents.

"I made a good living at it," Bowman said. "This was before they took the woods down and then I couldn't hide anymore. They built the golf course, ran me off the property and out of a job."

Caddying was his main line of work anyway, and it became more of a calling when the still dried up. He began carrying bags at neighboring Augusta Country Club years before and also served as a gardener at the nearby Bon Air Hotel, where most of the Masters field would take residence for the week. Once, he was asked to give a playing lesson to an Augusta

Country Club visitor from New Jersey. The man insisted on paying a caddie fee and eventually the two played for the money, at the visitor's insistence. Bowman pocketed $175 and was promptly sidelined by the Augusta Country Club caddie master for two weeks.

Luckily, Bowman was downtown shortly thereafter and the manager of the new Augusta National Golf Club recognized him.

"Augusta National is opening tomorrow, what are you doing?" the manager asked.

"Nothing," Bowman replied.

"Be over there tomorrow morning and get all the good caddies you can find," the manager said.

Bright and early the next day, in December 1932, Bowman was the first caddie in line as the bags came out for the first informal rounds. Tommy Armour, the famed "Silver Scot," was the first bag grabbed by Bowman.

Arnold Palmer (*center,* smoking cigarette) and a group of caddies watch Ben Hogan tee off during a practice round for the 1960 Masters. (© Historic Golf Photos/Ron Watts Collection)

By January 1933, when the club held a formal opening, the caddies were adorned in the first uniforms. According to the January 13, 1933 edition of the *Augusta Chronicle*: "As the visitors come into the grounds, they will find awaiting them a horde of red-caped negro caddies," thereby beginning a long tradition of best-dressed caddies.

Bowman would never win on a bag in the Masters, but he did caddie for the famed Ben Hogan. And as all Augusta National caddies to follow over the years testified, with a gleam in their eyes, even players of the magnitude of Hogan should have listened more intently to their input.

"(Hogan) always said, 'I didn't listen to you. I could have won the Masters. I made one mistake by not listening to you,' " Bowman said. "Hogan got in trouble one year on the fifteenth hole. I told him he couldn't reach the green with a 4-iron. He went in the pond in front of it."

Bowman moved to the Boston area after World War II. He gave up caddying to father eight children and worked at the American Barrel Company in Chelsea, Massachusetts, and on construction jobs. He rarely returned to Augusta—"When I pick up and leave a place, I don't want to go back too soon," he said—and died at age eighty-nine in 1998.

But his caddying wisdom lives on every spring at Augusta National. Just listen to how he assessed the tournament in the 1990 interview:

"Do your scoring on the first nine," Bowman said. "On the back side, you're getting into Disneyland."

The Double Eagle Pair

There is little doubt that Gene Sarazen's double eagle on the par-5 fifteenth hole in the 1935 Masters is the tournament's most famous shot and the one that spurred the tournament on to major championship fame years later. What is debatable is the role that Sarazen's caddie, the aptly named Stovepipe, played in the famous shot.

Sarazen made his first appearance at the Augusta National Golf Club in 1935, the year after skipping the inaugural event because of a conflict with a trip to South America with Joe Kirkwood for a series of golf exhibitions. He was assigned a caddie upon arriving at the second Augusta National Invitation Tournament (changed to the Masters Tournament in 1939) and became quite pleased with Stovepipe.

Stovepipe wore a tall, battered silk hat that resembled a top hat or "stovepipe" hat while caddying. Rarely has his given name been divulged, maybe because it was the equally odd name, Thor Nordwall, like some sort of Norse god. A rare photograph, taken from a distance and a bit out of focus, is shown in Sarazen's 1950 autobiography, *Thirty Years Of Championship Golf*, as the duo share a big smile. Stovepipe is wearing his patented black hat and a white shirt covered by a jacket. Without the patented white jumpsuit, to be instituted over a decade later, there is no indication that this man was a caddie.

At well over six feet tall, a height that was increased with the unusual hat, he towered over the five-feet-five Sarazen. They gave the impression of a Mutt and Jeff tandem.

Stovepipe was described as very religious and spent much of his free time at an Augusta church.

"How are things going?" Sarazen, a former caddie himself, asked Stovepipe once.

"Not so good, Mr. Gene, not so good," Stovepipe pouted. "Collections were mighty poor today. We done got to win."

Thor Nordwall, better known as "Stovepipe" because of his unusual hat, and Gene Sarazen pose for a photograph in 1935, the year Sarazen made a double eagle on No. 15 in the final round and won the tournament in a playoff the following day. Stovepipe is the first caddie of renown in Augusta National and Masters circles. (Originally printed in *30 Years of Championship Golf*)

Sarazen's week of preparation in 1935 was full of championship promise with four unprecedented practice rounds. Having never seen Augusta National before, he scorched the course to total 17-under par and quickly became the tournament favorite.

Surely, Stovepipe was partly responsible for Sarazen's quick adjustment to the brand new Augusta National course. In the 1934 tournament, the current nine-hole configurations were switched, leaving the now-famous Amen Corner near the start of the golf course. Because morning frost in the valleys of the current tenth and eleventh fairways caused a delay in membership play, the nines were reversed to the modern setup, making the back nine famous and positioning Sarazen for his great shot. Sarazen did not take to Augusta National at first, thinking the layout was too simple. The design included drive-and-pitch tenth and eleventh holes, shortish back-nine par 5s, and a mere 120-yard sixteenth hole. So, Stovepipe offered Sarazen the support to conquer this new course, as evidenced by the excellent practice play.

But as the tournament days arrived, the weather became cool and rainy. After three rounds, Craig Wood was 7-under par, one in front of Olin Dutra, two ahead of Henry Picard, and three in front of Sarazen.

Sarazen came to the fifteenth, then a 485-yard par 5, standing 1-over par for the final round and three strokes behind Wood. In those days, the fifteenth was a very generic hole, with a wide-open driving area, only a stream guarding the green, not a pond, and no sand trap set on the right edge. The pairings also were not arranged according to placement in the tournament standings. Wood teed off at 1 P.M. with Picard, approximately an hour and one-half ahead of Sarazen. Wood sank a long birdie putt on the final green to complete his round at 6-under-par 282. The press and tournament officials were already congratulating him on winning the title.

Sarazen, paired with Walter Hagen in the next-to-last group of the day, was walking to his tee shot on No. 15 as Wood finished. Hagen, on the way to a 79, was anxious to complete the round because he said he had a big date planned for the evening. The atmosphere was quite casual, as the players talked about old times, the tricks they used to play on each other, and, of course, Hagen and his women. Joe Williams, the New York newspaper columnist, walked alongside the pairing before bolting to the clubhouse just as he got word that Wood had finished.

"Well, I've seen enough of you bums," Williams said as he strolled off. "I'm going up to see the winner."

Bobby Jones, the Augusta National Golf Club and Masters cofounder, had walked down from the clubhouse to watch his friends complete their round. Byron Nelson, in the group ahead, was coming up the seventeenth fairway.

Hagen, having nothing to lose, played first to the fifteenth green. His approach shot with a 3-wood flew left of the green and beaned one of the approximately twenty spectators who surrounded the green—a man who had apparently had too much to drink—leaving the gallery laughing.

As Hagen's shot stirred the gallery, Sarazen was studying his approach shot. At first, he asked Stovepipe how he stood.

"What do I need to win?" Sarazen asked.

"You mean to beat Craig Wood, boss?" Stovepipe said.

Sarazen nodded. Stovepipe groaned.

"You need four threes, Mister Gene. Three, three, three, three."

Stovepipe apparently suggested that Sarazen lay up as they assessed their strategy.

"He wanted me to play it safe," Sarazen said in 1995. "He was a minister in town. He told me the money bag was very short (at church), so I should play it safe."

Sarazen finally won out and he and Stovepipe discussed club selection. Stovepipe wanted to pull a 3-wood to avoid the creek in front of the green at all costs. Sarazen was worried about his poor lie, so he chose the new Wilson Turf Rider 4-wood, his own invention that was in his bag, a club reminiscent of today's utility woods and one with which he could propel the ball higher in the air to fly over the hazard.

The ball flew just short of the green, bounced up on the putting surface and curled from right to left into the hole as the handful of people—thousands claimed to have seen it over the years—howled in delight. Sarazen had achieved Stovepipe's "3-3-3-3" with one swing, then parred in to tie with Wood and defeated him in a thirty-six-hole play-off the following day.

When Sarazen completed his play-off victory over Wood, he wondered how Augusta National would commemorate his famous shot of the previous day. Probably jokingly, he asked Stovepipe sometime the week after the tournament if he had heard any rumors of plans for a marker to be placed at the spot of his 4-wood second shot.

"Mister Gene," Stovepipe began, "they went down there this morning, some of the greenskeepers, I mean, and they done sprinkled a little rye seed in the divot and covered it up."

Sarazen was a bit despondent about how much Augusta National chairman Clifford Roberts tried to take advantage of the miracle shot. Roberts asked Sarazen to pose for publicity photographs on the fifteenth hole and to appear on the Rudy Vallee radio show the following year and held a contest in 1955 where pros tried to duplicate the double eagle. All of this and only a $1,500 first-place prize. Sarazen even lamented the measly $50 bonus he and Wood each received for playing the thirty-six extra holes of the play-off on Monday.

"I had to give Stovepipe more than that," Sarazen said.

And so goes the story of the first prominent player-caddie relationship in Masters history.

Pappy Stokes: The Godfather

The wiry, old man is just finishing breakfast, a dish of his favorite oatmeal, bacon, and toast with orange juice on the side. If the hired help at the "Your Home Sweet Home" assisted living facility is not paying attention, he will pick at the main course and go right for the sweets, or bang on his plate with his fork if the good stuff is tardy. This is a man whose sweet tooth is insatiable.

On this spring morning, however, the meal is secondary. He has been called from the kitchen table to meet someone. He rises slowly from the wooden kitchen chair, unfolding his long legs slowly to stand quietly and acknowledge the visitor who has arrived early on this Saturday. His sad eyes study the stranger as he shuffles smoothly from the kitchen, down a dark hallway and into the den to sit and talk about old times.

Normally, with a full stomach, his attention span wanes and he will return to his room for a nap. But when informed that the topic this morning is caddying in the Masters, the eyes of an eighty-three-year-old man brighten. He straightens his back to attention, raising his height to more than six feet tall, and has a sudden pep in his step and raised volume in his voice. He is told that this is the morning of the third round of the Masters Tournament. It is as if he is in his twenties again.

"I was the best caddie they ever had at the Masters," Willie "Pappy" Stokes exclaims, unsolicited. "I made all the money, a sack of money. I had nothing but money.

"And I had five women; took care of five women. And they were happy. Yes sir, I kept them all going."

The life of Pappy Stokes spans the entire time line of the Augusta National Golf Club. He was raised on the grounds of the Fruitland Nurseries before Bobby Jones and Clifford Roberts even knew about the property. He worked for four different Masters champions in five separate title runs, including Ben Hogan twice, over a fifteen-year span. Pappy also survived a lifelong battle with "drinkin', smokin' and womanizin'," as he puts it, to live a long, long life.

He is widely recognized in Augusta National caddie circles as the man who taught most of the "name" caddies how to read the undulating greens at Augusta National, to figure the

Willie "Pappy" Stokes lives in an assisted living home in downtown Augusta. Pictured in 2002, Stokes is considered the godfather of all Masters caddies, having won five times as a Masters caddie with four different players. (Photograph by Michael Holahan, © *Augusta Chronicle*)

wind as it swept through the trees behind the twelfth green, and the ins and outs of keeping your golfer focused and loose during the round in progress. He clubbed players by feel and sight, not via a yardage book. Iron Man, Willie Peterson, Ernest Nipper, and Carl Jackson were among his students. He was the wise old chief who taught all of the young braves the lay of the land.

"Pappy knew something that nobody else knew," says Carl Jackson, a disciple of Stokes in the early 1960s. "Many people know eighty-five percent of the putts out here, but the other fifteen percent they don't know. He told me, but I'm not telling. He taught me everything about this golf course."

Ask Pappy the secret to reading the greens and he gets introspective and serious. He first tells you he used just his memory to recall distances for clubbing and the breaks on the greens. His long, bony fingers become active, softly rubbing the imaginary surface of the green as he explains his learning process.

"I could tell which way the greens break just by looking at the golf course," he says. "Just look at it. Feel it with my hands to tell which way the grain runs. Nobody told me how, I just learned it myself. When I watched the man putt, I just watched the ball and remembered."

"He could be in the middle of a fairway," Jackson recalls, "look up at the green and say a certain putt was going to break six inches to the right."

Familiarity with the rolling hills of the Augusta National property was born to the Stokes family. Latimer Stokes Sr., his father, was originally an employee at the local dairy. Then he transitioned into work at Fruitland Nurseries with plants and in the various greenhouses on the property. Many of the assortment of plants that beautify the course today were the result of the handiwork of the Berckmans family, who owned the property, and workers such as Latimer Sr., who helped cultivate the exotic trees and plants that were imported from all over the world.

Belgian Baron Louis Mathieu Edouard Berckmans, a horticulturist by hobby, purchased the land in 1857 that was once an indigo plantation. He teamed with his son Prosper Julius Alphonse, an agronomist and horticulturist by profession, beginning in 1858. They developed one of the largest nurseries in the world that became what is claimed to be the first commercial nursery in the South. A great number of flowering plants and trees are still prominent at Augusta National today, including the long row of sixty-one magnolias, planted in the 1850s, that adorns Magnolia Lane and a plant that Prosper Berckmans popularized called the azalea, which is the signature beauty symbol on the grounds and in much of the South. Louis, Prosper's son, helped rehabilitate the plants when the course was completed and later joined with Jones and Roberts to determine which plants would be planted on each hole and thus have the hole named for that particular plant.

Latimer raised a family in a home on the edge of the property, probably somewhere in the vicinity of Washington Road, which was a dirt road in those days. The five children included Rupert, the oldest daughter, who was born in 1915; Willie, born on May 22, 1920; Garrett, born in 1923; Gussie Mae, born in 1930; and Latimer Jr., the baby, born in 1936. Rupert recalls that they moved from nearby Lincolnton, Georgia, to just across the street from Augusta National in the late 1910s, just before Fruitland Nurseries became defunct in 1918. For a time, as a youngster, she served as a maid for the Berckmans family who resided in the Old Manor House, now the central part of the Augusta National clubhouse. All the siblings, except for Garrett, who passed away in 1977, were in good health as of the summer of 2003. Long lives are a tradition in the Stokes family, as Latimer Sr. died at age eighty-six in 1981.

"I'm just happy God spared me and all of us this long," says eighty-eight-year-old Rupert Jones, who still enjoys volunteer work five days a week from 7 to 11 A.M. at Augusta's Veterans Administration Hospital. "And thank God for letting Pappy get as old as he's gotten."

Rupert remembers Pappy being laid back even as a little boy. He earned the nickname Pappy then because he was "always moving slow and unconcerned."

In the late 1920s, part of the Fruitland Nurseries property

was utilized as a farm and Pappy helped plow for planting of cotton and corn. Jones and Roberts purchased Fruitland Nurseries property to build their dream golf course in 1931. One year later, there was little eleven-year-old Pappy among the workers who were clearing trees and planning the routing of the course. He served as the water boy for the construction workers, toting the bucket around the woods to give them some needed refreshment. He remembers workers cutting down trees to clear the routing of the current tenth and eleventh holes. In all probability, this is where he learned the lay of the land for his future profession. He watched the water from rainstorms drain toward the lowest part of the property where Rae's Creek flows. He studied how the mules pulling equipment to mold the land for the golf course created subtle angles in the earth.

"I was born on the golf course, born and raised on the golf course," Pappy says. "Washington Road used to almost come right through my yard."

When Augusta National opened in December 1932 and then held its formal opening in January 1933, twelve-year-old Pappy jumped into the mix as a caddie, much to the chagrin of his father.

"When we were growing up, Pappy would skip school and go caddie," Rupert remembers. "And Daddy sure would get a hold of him for that. You know what he got? A big whipping. Daddy talked to him about going to school and didn't want him mixing with some of those caddies. But Pappy had his mind made up what he was going to do. He wanted to be a caddie. Even when he got older, when he was working in construction on homes, when it came time to caddie he went right to the golf course. That's mostly all he did his whole life."

By age seventeen, Pappy already had won a Masters title as a caddie. In 1938, the last tournament called the Augusta National Invitation Tournament, Henry Picard never shot above par, finished at 3-under-par 285 and two in front of "Lighthorse" Harry Cooper and Ralph Guldahl for by far his most prominent golf moment.

World War II called next and Pappy fought for the Army

in the Pacific theater beside white men, just as he worked beside them as an Augusta National caddie. By this time, he had also married, to Odella, Iron Man's older sister.

When Pappy came back from battle, the opportunity to caddie was still there. He did not know another trade, so why not return to something he was born to do? His next successful bag was that of Claude Harmon, a club professional who had never won a PGA Tour tournament. Harmon would later become famous as the father of Tiger Woods' coach, Butch Harmon, and three other professional sons at some of the top clubs in the country.

In 1948, Harmon practiced with Hogan at his winter golf club job, Seminole Golf Club in Palm Beach, Florida, in preparation for the Masters. As a part of his usual spring routine, Harmon would drive north and stop in Augusta for the Masters at about the halfway point of his journey. He would play in good friend Bobby Jones' tournament, visit with an assortment of pros, and then take off the next week for the rest of the trip to his winter post as the head professional at the famed Winged Foot Golf Club in Mamaroneck, New York.

However, this week would set up differently for the Savannah, Georgia, native. After regularly beating Hogan on his home course in the practice rounds, including firing a course-record 60 at Seminole, Harmon proceeded to equal the 9-under-par 279 Masters tournament record for a five-stroke victory over Cary Middlecoff. He became the first native Georgian to win the tournament.

This good-luck charm of a caddie was not lost on some of the game's more promising players, particularly Hogan. He had become the bridesmaid of the Masters, with eight consecutive top-ten finishes dating back to 1939, his second year in the tournament. That included back-to-back runner-up finishes where he should have won. Fort Worth, Texas, childhood friend and rival Byron Nelson played the final thirteen holes 5-under par in an eighteen-hole play-off in 1942 to nip Hogan 69-70. After World War II, in the 1946 Masters, Hogan rallied from five back entering the final round, only to three-putt for bogey from twelve feet above the hole on the super-fast eighteenth green to lose by one to journeyman Herman Keiser.

"Congratulations, Herman," Picard told Keiser in the club-house after Hogan's three-putt. "The Little Man (Hogan) really took the choke. Those were the three worst putts I've ever seen him hit."

As Hogan prepared for the 1951 Masters, he searched for a new caddie for the practice rounds. Augusta National's wide-open driving areas and severely undulating, fast greens did not suit Hogan's precise driving skills and limited his aggressive iron play, but he was out to prove a point. Hogan arrived ten days before the tournament began to study the course and pound hundreds of balls from the right side of the old practice range, with Pappy shagging balls in the distance, moving only to avoid being beaned by another player's ball. Pappy had won on two different bags, and Hogan was a longtime pal of Harmon. Pappy quickly recognized Hogan's eagle-eye focus.

"Mr. Hogan, you play pretty good and you could win the Masters if your caddie helped you any," Pappy said.

"Yep, we'll see. I want you to work for me during the tournament," Hogan replied.

That hiring immediately evoked a response from Harmon when he arrived at the tournament.

"Hey Ben, you've got my caddie!" Harmon yelled.

"Yeah I'm gonna keep him," Hogan blurted back as he turned to Pappy.

To finalize the hiring, Hogan immediately gave Pappy a twenty dollar bill and told him to go buy some lunch. That was a huge tip in those days for even the wealthiest players and especially before the tournament even began.

"I still might have been caddying for Claude Harmon if it wouldn't have been for that twenty dollars," Pappy says. "I took that money and went to get a drink of liquor and something to eat right after Hogan gave it to me."

Hogan began a great four-year run with a win in the 1951 Masters, shooting a final-round four-birdie, no-bogey 68 to beat Skee Riegel by two strokes. Two years later, once again with

Pappy on the bag, Hogan set the tournament record of 14-under-par 274 to take home the first of three major championship titles in 1953. A windblown final-round 79 in 1952, complete with five three-putts after he was tied with Sam Snead for the third-round lead, and a 70-71 play-off loss to Snead in 1954 kept Hogan from winning four consecutive Masters.

"Ben Hogan made fun of your course, didn't he, Cliff?" President Dwight D. Eisenhower joked with Cliff Roberts two days after the 1953 tournament when Hogan joined them for a casual round.

Ben Hogan chips to the second green on the way to winning his first Masters title in 1951. Willie "Pappy" Stokes (left) earned his third Masters title as a caddie with Hogan and would win again in 1953 with Hogan. (AP/Wide World Photos)

It was during this time that Hogan perfected much of his strategy on how to attack a golf course, particularly Augusta National. There is no account that Hogan consulted with Pappy in this area, especially seeing that Hogan was a lone wolf on the golf course in determining his blueprint for a round. "Hogan always talked to his caddie, but it was always about anything but golf," recalls Jack Burke Jr., the 1956 Masters champion and a compatriot of Hogan's in the 1950s. But, consider that Pappy and Hogan have long been anointed as the ultimate tacticians of their professions. Also, remember that Hogan, nicknamed "The Hawk" for his ability to break down a course, was introduced to golf as a caddie at Glen Garden Country Club in Fort Worth.

"No yardage man; he was the best at pulling a club by eye," longtime Augusta National caddie master Freddie Bennett said of Pappy.

"I don't know the yardage; I didn't want to know the yardage," Hogan once said. "There are too many variables—the wind, the air density, how you're playing that day. I would remember if I had been beside a certain tree or trap or something like that and what I hit and how I played that shot. I don't think I could play by yardage."

Therefore, here is how Hogan learned to play the devilish par-3 twelfth hole at Augusta National, famous for its swirling winds that have blown many a tee shot into Rae's Creek, which guards the front of the green. It was the only place where Hogan's preshot routine varied. Instead of his standard couple of waggles with the club before beginning his takeaway, he would waggle until "I felt the wind on my cheek and, therefore, the flag (on No. 12) would be up, the wind would be consistent, it would be normal—instead of coming up or dropping down."

Who else but Hogan, partnered with Pappy's inherent knowledge of the course, could figure out such a complex strategy?

Hogan also tested unusual ways to play Augusta National's key holes during this era. In 1951, he regularly began playing his approach shot directly to the right of the par-4 eleventh green to avoid the newly built pond, added in 1950, that tightly guards the left side of the green. "If I hit that green, you know it's a mistake," he said. He also practiced a knockdown shot for the par-3 sixteenth hole and developed guidelines for when to go for greens in two shots on the par-5 thirteenth and fifteenth holes.

In the years following this unprecedented Masters run, Hogan was reaching his early forties and his putting was becoming a severe handicap. "I'm not afraid of missing the putt. I'm afraid I can't draw the putter back. When I look at the cup, it's filled with my blood," Hogan lamented. That was something that not even Pappy could help cure.

Pappy's last hurrah came in 1956 when Burke rallied from a record eight strokes back in the final round to beat Ken Venturi by one stroke.

Burke's winning score of 1-over-par 289 is still the highest winning score in tournament history (tied with the 289 of Hogan and Snead in 1954) causing tournament cofounder Jones to call 1956 "the hardest playing conditions we've ever had in this tournament." High winds rushed through the course during most of the tournament, resulting in a record eighty-seven rounds of 80 or higher. That was culminated by twenty-nine scores of 80 or higher on Sunday, including amateur Charles Kunkle's high-water mark of 95, still the highest single score in Masters history.

The wind was such a factor that in the second round Bob Rosburg, now a veteran ABC-TV broadcaster, suffered an embarrassing occurrence. With a stiff, 40 mph wind in his face on the par-3 twelfth hole, Rosburg chose a 4-iron on the 155-yard hole. Just as he slammed his ball into the wind, the gale force ceased completely and the ball flew the fronting Rae's Creek, the green, the bunkers, the woods behind, and into neighboring Augusta Country Club—out of bounds and nearly twenty-five yards over the green. Rosburg shook his head in disbelief, re-teed, and with the consistent wind, played to within ten feet.

Burke and Venturi also experienced the wind tunnel on the long par-3 fourth hole. Venturi used a driver into the wind on the then-220-yard hole and ended up ten yards over the green. Burke also used a driver and finished sixty yards short of the green.

The 1956 association with Burke may have been Pappy's finest hour as a caddie. Burke had failed to win a major championship to that point. He had learned the game under the tutelage of his father, a renowned teaching pro, and another star Texan, three-time Masters winner Jimmy Demaret. Later in his career, he even served as assistant pro to Claude Harmon at the Thunderbird Country Club in Palm Springs, California. Jackie had shot 69 at age twelve, qualified for the U.S. Open at age sixteen, and turned pro at age nineteen. His career highlights had occurred in assembling an unbeaten record in three previous Ryder Cup appearances and a stellar 1952 season, where he totaled five victories and four in a row at the Texas Open, Houston Open, Baton Rouge Open, and St. Petersburg Open in consecutive weeks. But the thirty-three-year-old Burke had not won since 1953, mainly because his trusty putting was letting him down, some of that attributable to the fact that his favorite putter had been stolen a few years before and he could not get comfortable with a replacement. In 1955, Burke held the first-round lead in the Masters, but floundered with a final-round 80 and finished thirteenth. Some also thought his serious attitude on the course needed to be softened. That, plus he had priorities at home.

"I choose to spend a good proportion of my time with my wife and our kids because twenty years from now I'd like to have a few other things in my life than just the joy of being recognized when I walk into a restaurant," Burke said in the mid-1950s.

Burke was interested in having a caddie who would simply join him for a walk around the course. Augusta National member Phil Harison, the official first-tee starter since 1948 who is still manning that position today, helped pair Burke and Pappy, of course, with the consent of Clifford Roberts.

"I didn't want a caddie on the green or on top of my golf ball," Burke recalls today. "I needed some air out there. I didn't need a Stanford graduate to tell me how to play like the guys on Tour do today. Sometimes the players and caddies today look like they're preparing for an economic meeting the way they study every shot. Any dumbass would know that everything at Augusta National breaks toward Rae's Creek, so I didn't think I needed much help.

"Pappy was very good. He never got upset. He had an even keel. That's why a lot of players liked Pappy. Things were never as bad as they seemed or as good as they seemed with him."

As the final round began, amateur Ken Venturi led by four over Cary Middlecoff, seven over Doug Ford, and eight over Burke and Lloyd Mangrum. Only a disaster could lead to Venturi's downfall or a miracle to Burke's uprising. Burke's goal was to finish second and win the $6,000 first-place prize money given to the low professional.

It was the first time CBS televised the Masters, with cameras covering the action from the fifteenth green to the finishing hole from Friday's second round to Sunday's finale. The drama during the final round was more like a U.S. Open. Instead of the patented back-nine Augusta shoot-out, the question was who would be the last man standing on another windblown day.

"When I got up that morning I thought there's no way anybody's going to break 100 around here," Burke says. "You just had to be ready for five or six hours of torture."

Burke and Pappy glided around the course for a final-round 71, joining Snead's 71 as the only sub-par rounds on the final day. Burke used his patented popping putting stroke to record only twenty-nine putts that day and had just one three-putt the entire tournament. Obviously, he had regained his putting touch. Venturi skied to an 80 and Middlecoff to a 77, clearing the way for an improbable victor.

The key moment occurred on the par-4 seventeenth. Burke trailed Venturi, playing behind him, and Middlecoff, just in front of him, by one stroke entering the straightaway par 4. Middlecoff made double bogey after duffing a chip from the front edge and three-putting. Burke played an 8-iron to within fifteen feet of a tricky hole position just behind the front bunker. The path to the hole was strewn with sand that had been blown out of the greenside bunker by the 30 mph winds. Using his boyhood experience of putting on sand greens in Texas, Burke recollected that sand makes a green putt much faster. At first glance, he thought the putt was going to stop halfway to the hole but it kept moving and finally skidded in for a birdie. "It was one of the few balls that even stayed on that green all day," Burke says.

Playing partner Mike Souchak, the stocky former Duke University football player, embraced Burke as they walked off the seventeenth green toward the eighteenth hole. "C'mon, man," Souchak shouted. "They're still making bogeys out here. Let's go."

Sure enough, Venturi's approach to seventeen was long and he made bogey to put Burke one stroke up. When Venturi parred eighteen, Burke had won his first major title and rode the momentum to capture the 1956 PGA Championship and earn PGA Player of the Year honors. That season also enabled Burke to join Demaret in 1958 to build their dream course in Houston, Champions Golf Club, one of the nation's most respected courses. By 2000, Burke had been elected to the World Golf Hall of Fame.

As usual, the caddie accounts of Burke's surprise victory give more credit to their input.

"Mr. Roberts told (Burke) whatever Pappy tells you, you do it," says longtime Augusta National caddie "Pee Wee" Reid.

"I just told him all he's got to do is hit the ball," Pappy remembers. "Shut your eyes when you walk up to the ball. I'll tell you what to hit. I picked the club. If I gave him the right club, it gave him confidence that he could play the course. He could go on and play his game then and not worry about misclubbing long or short.

"On Sunday on eighteen, we were walking up the fairway and Jack Burke Jr. just said, 'How much money do you want?' He picked me up and he was much littler than I was. He asked me again how much money I wanted. I just told him a sack full."

Pappy was so assured that Burke would make a great come-back that he made a quick wager the morning of the final round.

"I bet a man at the package shop in downtown Augusta that we were gonna win that tournament against Ken Venturi," Pappy says. "The man just laughed at me. He finally said, 'Pappy, you're eight strokes behind. If you win that tournament I'll give you a gallon of liquor.'

"After Jack Burke Jr. came back to win, I went downtown late that afternoon, walked into the package shop and saw the man. All I said was, 'Here I is.' "

Burke was impressed, but not enough to recall Pappy's name: "I don't know what my caddie's last name is. Just call him Willie Burke," Burke told the press after winning.

Nearly fifty years later, Burke's recollection focused solely on the confidence that Pappy instilled in players. He did not know until years later that Pappy had caddied for a succession of champions even though Pappy worked with Burke for much of the late 1950s.

"On eighteen, I hit my second shot in a bunker and blasted out to about five feet," says Burke, who turned eighty-one in January. "I was as nervous as a cat on a hot tin roof, so I needed to talk to somebody. I read the putt and finally asked Pappy, 'Is it inside the left edge?' That's the only time I asked him the line. I just wanted to be sure. He just nodded his head and said, 'Just cruise it in there for us, just cruise it in.'

"Pappy was very alert all the time. Nothing got by him. He had great timing and a sense of balance. You could always tell a guy who had a great sense of feel by the way he walked. Like Snead. They both had a great stride as if they would never stumble no matter where they were walking. Pappy was very easy to work with. The ball was clean, the clubs were clean and he never bitched about anything. He never needed any money or bugged me about getting paid. I would do anything for my caddie. It was just sometimes I didn't want them to do anything for me."

No matter what Pappy's influence was during play, it cannot be argued that he made an impact on the men with whom he won. Picard, Harmon, Hogan, Demaret, and Burke never won a Masters before or after Pappy carried their bags.

By the 1960s, Pappy had become The Godfather for the caddies. He worked for various members and tutored many of the young caddies. If he saw caddies in his group or those nearby clowning around, Pappy was quick with a harsh word about straightening up.

"If you were lackadaisical, Pappy would say, 'God's got his eyes on you,' " Reid says.

"I didn't go out there on the golf course to play," Pappy says. "I went out there to try to make a living. Some of them couldn't caddie; they were just bag toters. They never did nothing but tote a bag."

But he could also add some levity to the situation.

"You couldn't help but like him," "Buck" Moore says. "He was comical off the course. He'd always say something funny if you had a bad day to pep you up."

What was not funny was that Pappy could not loop anymore. He was getting too old.

"The last time I caddied, I went out there and couldn't even get up the hill on eighteen," he says. "I'd had enough when that happened."

Pappy's livelihood away from the golf course was similar to that of many of the Augusta National caddies. They became quasi-celebrities in town and had a little pocket change from their caddie wages. Many, like Iron Man, would splurge on new cars. Pappy once crossed the Savannah River into South Carolina, where the car deals were more appealing, and purchased a new Chevrolet. But he favored a simple drink of whiskey.

"You could make seventy-five cents per eighteen holes in the old days," Pappy says. "That was a lot of money then. I would have caddied three times a day if I could have. And whiskey was fifteen cents a half pint."

By the 1980s, Pappy was what many called a "happy drunk." In 1985, he faced sixty days in the Richmond County Jail for a drunken driving change. For a short period of time, he lived on the streets, calling himself "Pete the Tramp." He lived in a variety of homes where he eventually had to leave because of his drinking, carousing, and inability to pay rent. His family tried to help, but Pappy's stubborn will prevailed. Many of his old caddie associates lost track of him.

Finally, in the late 1990s, as he approached age eighty, Pappy found a home at "Your Home Sweet Home," a simple assisted-living home located on Martin Luther King Jr. Boulevard near downtown Augusta. The worn, wood-framed house blends in with the residential neighborhood and no signs indicate this is a retirement facility. Pappy shares the home with a handful of elderly black people, none as old or peppy as Pappy. His vision and hearing are not as good as they used to be, and he has arthritis. Still, Kathleen Beasley, the owner of the home, enjoys hearing stories about how this old man with a checkered recent history has transformed into a docile character with a glorious early life.

"I quit smoking and I quit drinking a few years ago," Pappy says. "I just threw my glass away, broke it."

Pappy's baby brother, Latimer Jr., comes by weekly to give him a haircut. Rupert, his older sister, visits to chat and cut his fingernails and toenails. Jack Stephens, the former chairman of the Augusta National Golf Club, has sent a $100 Christmas gift before. Some old-time caddies stop by periodically to just say hello. Tom Van Dorn, the Augusta National caddie master, has voiced an interest in getting him back out to Augusta National as part of a reunion of the old caddies.

If he ever returns to Augusta National, you could truly say it would be a sweet homecoming.

Cemetery and Ike:
The Executive Connection

Mention the name Willie Frank Perteet and you get little response, a blank stare. But invoke the name of President Dwight D. Eisenhower and the nickname "Cemetery" and you discover an instant celebrity.

Perteet was Eisenhower's regular caddie at Augusta National when Ike became a member of the club in 1948 until 1957, a period when the thirty-fifth president of the United States led the national popularization of the game. Coupled with the emergence of Arnold Palmer late in the 1950s, they caused an even greater wave in the sport. In 1948, the National Golf Foundation listed 2.8 million golfers who played at least fifteen times annually. By 1969, when Eisenhower died, there were well over 10 million golfers. The sport was making a transition from a recreational activity for the wealthy into a more accessible pastime.

Eisenhower's history in Augusta is quite abundant. The Eisenhower Pine, more commonly called Ike's Tree, is the tall loblolly pine that guards the left side of the fairway on the par-4 seventeenth hole. Eisenhower, who fought a slice in his golf game, all too often pulled his tee shot into the tree and saw it rattle around and drop to the ground. He once requested to Augusta National Chairman Clifford Roberts that the tree be chopped down. Roberts avoided addressing the issue during a club meeting by quickly adjourning the gathering. Ike's Pond, which occupies three acres on the Par-3 Course, was named for the president in the late 1940s after he suggested to Roberts that it would making a nice fishing hole. The Eisenhower Cabin, also called "Mamie's Cabin" after the first lady, was the first of ten cabins built for members. The structure, which stands left of the tenth fairway, was built in 1953 for $150,000 and funded by the Augusta National membership to house the president on his visits to Augusta. Reid Memorial Presby-

President Dwight D. Eisenhower *(right)* and caddie Willie "Cemetery" Perteet pose from the President's golf cart at Augusta National in 1953. Perteet often had a difficult assignment working for Ike because the President played at a particularly quick pace and was often escorted by Secret Servicemen, one with a Thompson machine gun hidden in a golf bag. (© Historic Golf Photos/Ron Watts Collection)

terian Church, located on Walton Way, was the regular Sunday worship site for the Eisenhowers when they visited Augusta. Their usual up-front church pew is adorned with a gold plaque. A stained-glass window with a likeness of the president memorializes his visits.

And there was Perteet right in the middle of it all, being interviewed for national magazine and newspaper articles and radio broadcasts.

Perteet was a slight man, five-feet-six, 135 pounds, who got his start caddying in the Masters at a relatively old age, thirty-two, in 1936. He was in his mid forties when he began caddying for Ike. His nickname was originally "Dead Man," until Ike decided to make it simpler.

"All dead men belong in cemeteries," Ike said, "so from now on I'll call you Cemetery."

Perteet came by his macabre nickname in a frightening, yet humorous, manner. Various accounts over the years stated that he was caught in bed with a woman when her boyfriend came home and took a knife to him, with Cemetery suffering only minor wounds. But, in a 1953 *Life* magazine story, Perteet gave a more detailed story.

In the early 1920s, in his late teens, Perteet broke off a longtime relationship with a young girl because he said he loved another.

"I explained honestly why I couldn't marry her," Perteet said. "And I thought that was the end of it. But not with that girl. She got two friends and them three waited for me with knives outside a place where I was drinking beer. It was dark when I came out and I didn't see them. And they laid aboard me. They didn't miss. Cut me up real bad. I started running, them after me, yelling like she-devils. I didn't yell, man. I was saving my breath. I run to a taxi stand, and a cabbie took me to the hospital. That was on a Monday night.

"They must have given me too much ether when they wanted to operate. Leastways, that's my opinion. And I went off into a trance, like, for four days and they finally thought I was dead. They took me to a room in the morgue for an inquest on Thursday. Few minutes before the inquest I suddenly rose up, and that orderly ain't been seen 'round town since. Everybody say I cheated the cemetery so that's how come they all call me 'Cemetery' or 'Dead Man' 'round here."

Perteet was also noted as the leader of a local jazz band

Willie "Cemetery" Perteet split his time between caddying for President Dwight D. Eisenhower and drumming for local Augusta bands during his heyday of the 1950s. Perteet may have become the most famous Augusta National caddie because of his association with President Eisenhower during the 1950s. (© Historic Golf Photos/Ron Watts Collection)

that entertained around the area. Perteet played the drums, usually sporting a dress coat, white shirt, and black bowtie, as the band played tunes such as "Chattanooga Choo Choo." Perteet publicly lauded his lead singer, a tenor named Teddy Adams: "Man, he's solid!" Perteet said. He occasionally played with Clarence Pinckney, a famous name among 1950's musicians because of the formation of The Drifters. Perteet also was known for his singing, particularly a comic rendition of "Who Stole the Lock off the Hen House Door?"

"I've been playing music for some kind of money almost as long as I was a head high to a drum," Perteet said. "That's breath of life to me."

Mostly, the band played for predominantly white crowds—many times until 1 A.M.—that grew larger when Perteet began caddying for Eisenhower. Once, in 1953, the president flew in late from Washington to play golf at Augusta National. He changed clothes immediately and quickly played seven holes until darkness fell, retiring to a bridge game with fellow Augusta National members. As a result, Perteet was late for his gig at Rich's Club on Sand Bar Ferry Road in south Augusta.

"I apologize to you folks for being late 'cause I know you-all been waiting for me to play," Perteet announced to the crowd upon arriving after the band had played a few tunes. "But, ladies and gentlemen, I been unavoidably detained by the President of the United States."

Aside from his brush with death and late hours as a musician, Perteet was deemed reliable by none other than John Henry "Eleven" Williams, the caddie master at Augusta National until the late 1950s.

"For somebody as important as General Eisenhower, I knew I had to get him a reliable caddie," Williams said. "None of the no-count boys we got so frequently applyin' for caddie jobs 'round here, some of them smelling just like they come out of a whiskey barrel. Cemetery now—he's mature. He's got sense. And he plays golf. Does right well in the caddie matches in the evenings after the members get off the fairways. Knows the course and he knows his clubs.

"So I give the General Cemetery. 'Cemetery,' I say, 'you do

right well out here, you hear?' When the General come back, I say, 'General, how do you like that boy I give you?' An' the general say, 'Eleven, he was fine.' So him and Cemetery been together ever since."

Willie "Cemetery" Perteet, pictured in the 1970s, worked for President Dwight D. Eisenhower in the 1950s. He was often given Masters Week off to rest up for President Eisenhower's visit to Augusta the week after the tournament. (© *Augusta Chronicle*)

Perteet became quite a celebrity for his relationship with the president. In 1953, *Life* featured him in its May 11 issue, pictured caddying and behind his drum set. He was withheld from the normal Masters Tournament caddie rotation for a few years so that he would be fresh for Ike's usual arrival after the tournament. On many occasions, Ike would play on consecutive days, including a tee time with the just-jacketed Masters champion.

"I wouldn't say he was no pillar of the community," one person in the Augusta black community said of Perteet, "but he's well known, no doubt about that, and especially since he and the president been connected."

Eisenhower was not the greatest golfer, just the most famous. Cemetery recounted years later that the best score Ike ever shot was a 78, playing the members' tees during a round with Arnold Palmer. According to Roberts, Eisenhower broke 80 four times during forty-five trips to Augusta National over a seventeen-year span that included twenty-nine visits and 210 rounds while he was in office. Eisenhower was bothered by a knee injury suffered during his days as a football player at the U.S. Military Academy at West Point. He swung mostly with his upper body, did not generate much power, and sliced the ball. He was also a poor putter, often stroking putts before his caddie could consult with him on the break. Playing partners would occasionally concede difficult putts to Ike because they felt sorry for his poor putting ability.

Perteet did not reveal details on Ike's golf game until after Ike passed away in 1969.

"Mr. Ike was a pretty good golfer," Cemetery said in 1970. "He wasn't no Nicklaus, no blockbuster. When the pros use an iron, he'd use a 3- or 4-wood. But he kept the ball in play pretty good.

"One of the promises I made Mr. Ike was I'd never tell anybody what he paid me. Don't guess it makes much difference now. He used to give me ten dollars plus an extra dollar on Sunday for church. I remember one time he's down here for ten days and we're setting up and he says, 'My word, Cemetery, if this keeps up I'll be working for you.' "

Eisenhower's penchant for slipping out of the White House for numerous rounds of golf drew criticism from political rivals. His first trip after winning the 1952 Presidential election was a flight to Augusta National for a ten-day victory celebration with political aides and future Cabinet members. He had a putting green built in 1954—funded by private donations and designed by the United States Golf Association—just outside his White House office door on the South Lawn, much to the dismay of many Executive Office traditionalists. When squirrels damaged the green, the president joked that he wanted them shot, but some were eventually trapped and relocated. He often dictated letters in the Oval Office while swinging his favorite 8-iron. Many times, he would complete his hectic day by slipping on his golf shoes and then leave small cleat marks in the historic wooden floor as he walked, putter or wedge in hand, to view the South Lawn. On average, he played approximately thirty-six holes per week when at home in Washington. Many opponents questioned his dedication to the office because of his love of golf. When that did not faze the former general, they began to take potshots at his questionable golf ability.

As the 1956 presidential election approached, a campaign began—obviously from the rival Democratic Party—with a prominent bumper sticker, "Ben Hogan For President. If we're going to have a golfer, let's have a good one." That effort to demean Eisenhower did not work either. Later that year, *Golf Digest* began a campaign, with Ike's participation, where buttons were circulated saying, "Don't Ask What I Shot," endearing him to hackers nationwide who were taking up the game.

If he did not play well, at least Ike did not draw out the agony. Much like the golf-playing Bush family, a round of golf with Ike was more of a sprint than a marathon. He often played "ready golf," taking the tee out of turn before the rest of his group arrived. Political pundits in Washington, D.C., lamented that mid-week greens fees at Burning Tree Golf Club, the course of choice for government officials in the nation's capital, were made higher by Eisenhower to discourage play so that he could zoom around the course. Keeping up with the president may have been the most difficult task for Cemetery.

Ike was also very talkative, particularly with his caddie, and showed respect for any advice he dispensed. He also tipped more than normal, often handing out five dollars and two of his Dunlop Dot golf balls, engraved with "Mr. President." Cemetery recalled the day that Eisenhower pulled his drive into the left woods on No. 10, just down the hill from his namesake cottage. The ball was behind a log, prohibiting the president from swinging.

"Cemetery, do you think you are a man?" Ike asked loudly. "Well, come over here and help me move this log."

Cemetery put down the golf bag and sped over.

"The Secret Servicemen rushed over to help but Mr. Ike told them to get out of there and he got on one end of the log and me the other and he said, 'Lift!' and we picked it up and toted it ten feet away.

"He was a nice man. A very nice man. A very, very nice gentleman."

Cemetery caddied under unusual circumstances. The Secret Service would often station a man, carrying a Thompson submachine gun in a golf bag, in the same foursome. Once, a paparazzi hiding in the woods at Augusta National was nearly shot by the Secret Service because his photo equipment looked like a sniper's gun. Walkie-talkies were always available in case of a national crisis. Pinkerton security guards, utilized for Masters play, were also hired to scout the grounds when the president was on site. By 1953, Augusta National built a chain-link fence around its 365 acres to keep out trespassers, an addition that was a Secret Service suggestion later to become a necessity as the club became a national landmark. Cemetery had to rise early after his late-night band gigs to get to Augusta National by 8 A.M., in time to shag balls on the driving range as Ike warmed up and took lessons from head professional Ed Dudley.

Perteet may have been privy to classified information during Eisenhower's visits to Augusta National. He said the president rarely discussed policy with his playing partners, but the

Korean War was in progress and it was the start of the Cold War. You could sense Eisenhower's political temperature by his golf game: If a call came from Washington, Ike was often surly and played poorly. If the coast was clear, he was noticeably jovial and competitive. Perteet not only kept that information secret, if he knew anything, but everything else about Ike's private life.

"You heard all the secrets of the H-bomb. And how that is classified information—unfit for public information," Cemetery said in the early 1950s. "Well, so far as I is concerned, the General's golf score lately is just the same—classified information."

As the late 1950s came, Cemetery had reached his early fifties. Dudley opted to make a change on Eisenhower's bag because "Cemetery is getting a little decrepit" and that "it is advisable to give the president a younger and more alert man." In Cemetery's place was Slim Jenkins, a man in his mid-thirties.

"The President plays like a whirlwind," Dudley said. "He hits the ball and—swoosh—he's gone. It takes a young man to keep up with him. So I had to make a change."

Perteet was admittedly disappointed at the move.

"I'm not ready for the grave yet, even if they do call me Cemetery," Perteet said. "If anybody thinks so they should see me at the night club where I play drums at night. I can stand on my hands and walk to that first tee there. How many of these young squirts can do that?"

By 1964, Perteet was left out of the caddie roster for the Masters. He tried to get a bag but was late arriving and did not make the cut. At a mere 112 pounds, he was only a shadow of his former bubbly self, described as "looking like a scrawny bantam rooster." He was broke and did not even have his drumming work anymore.

The only thing left was the memory of being the right-hand man to the president, a title that few men in any profession could claim.

A Caddie's Letter

James L. "Baldy" Ricks was a caddie at the Augusta National Golf Club off and on from the mid-1940s until the late 1980s. During that time, Ricks served as the occasional caddie for future president Dwight D. Eisenhower, in the fall of 1950 when Eisenhower was president of Columbia University, and for players such as Bobby Jones, Chick Harbert, Dick Chapman, and Vic Ghezzi. Ricks attended high school at Haines Institute in Augusta before his family moved to Oklahoma. After graduating from high school in the Sooner state, Ricks went to Wilberforce University in Ohio, a rare college graduate among the Augusta National caddie ranks. He returned to Augusta in the mid-1950s to serve at Fort Gordon in the U.S. Army and continued his caddying. Even though he spent the majority of his career as a mail carrier in the U.S. Postal Service in Detroit, Michigan, and Beverly Hills, California, Ricks would trek back to Augusta every spring to caddie in the Masters. Scared of flying, he hopped a bus back for his spring homecoming.

Ricks retired from the U.S. Postal Service in 1999. Eighty years old and living in San Bernardino, California, he still comes back to Augusta annually to visit old friends, including former Augusta National caddie master Freddie Bennett. He wrote the following letter about his caddying experience to the *Augusta Chronicle* in the late 1990s. Most noteworthy is the brief encounter with Bobby Jones, one year after Jones played his last eighteen-hole round because of the early affects of syringomyelia, the disease that would eventually kill him.

The year was 1949. It was about midweek, 5 o'clock in the afternoon. I was sitting in the Old Caddy House waiting for a ride downtown. "Shorty," the driver, as well as a lot of the caddies, were engaged in card games called Koon Kang and Tonk, trying to increase their daily earnings before heading downtown to the watering hole on Broad Street called "Doc Norval's." While waiting, the Caddie Master came into the Caddie House and asked me if I would like to go a few holes. Naturally, I accepted because my chances of adding to my earnings were much better than playing cards with my quick-handed buddies.

As we walked back up to the clubhouse, waiting was Mr. Jones. I had seen him on several different occasions talking with Mr. (Clifford) Roberts but never up close. He asked me if I could drive a car. Immediately, I replied yes sir, so he put the clubs in the trunk and said drive me out to 15 tee. At that time, he had a green 1949 Cadillac. I got behind the wheel and drove down the service road parallel to the No. 1 hole. As I drove down behind the No. 1 green, to go down the hill on No. 2 toward the No. 15 tee, I turned the corner of the road but I didn't turn wide enough to prevent the rear wheels from going into the dirt in the middle of this narrow road. Mr. Jones smiled and said you had to allow for the break, turn your front wheels a little wider so your rear wheels will stay on the road. "Yes sir," I replied. We finally made it to 15 tee. He told me he was going to play 15, 16 and 17 which would bring us back to the car.

So he teed off on 15 with a fluid swing, not very far but accurate. He hit his second shot somewhat short of the creek that approached the green. He hit his third shot on the green. In the customary fashion of caddies, you always stay in front of the player. But when I got to the wooden bridge crossing the creek he yelled, "Wait up." He jokingly said if he fell in the water he was going to take me with him. There was a slight climb from the end of the bridge and up the embankment to the green, but needless to say we didn't go in. Sixteen was a "piece of cake," mostly level. Seventeen was a test, almost all uphill until passing the Eisenhower Tree on the left of the fairway. He completed the 17th hole, we got back into the car and I didn't drive into the middle isle on my return. He paid me and said "thanks." Naturally, I thanked him back for allowing me to (out) drive him.

As I looked back to my caddie's days at Augusta, which covered about 20 years, I am in awe of how caddying has changed. First, outside (Tour) caddies were not allowed, which gave the local caddies exclusive rights to the tournament. Most of the caddies and Caddie Master ("Eleven") had names we never knew. Pappy caddied for Hogan, Banny caddied for Demaret, Shorty caddied for Mangrum, Iron Man caddied for Palmer and there were often names like Cigarette, Round head, Nipper, Gardoolie, Cemetery and Shoo Poon. I ("Baldy") caddied for Chick Harbert. My nickname was given to me by Mr. (Ed) Dudley (the head professional). I, of course, thought he gave me this nickname because I ran very hard shagging balls when he would give golf lessons. Apparently, he saw something then that would become a part of my head dress in later years.

Caddies today are Mathematicians, Accountants, Professional Golfers, Globetrotters and Investors. Today, caddies don't linger nor memorize the cards, they chart the yards. It's big business, 10 % of the Golfer's earnings plus bonuses. Caddies earn more today in one year than the leading money winners from 1945 to 1965.

"Eleven" passed away and it was then that I found out his real name (John Williams). I owe him great thanks for allowing me to outdrive the only Grand Slammer in golf.

Billy (Baldy) Ricks

Fireball Gets Fired Up

The fifteenth hole is where Doug Ford won the 1957 Masters, whether Fireball liked it or not.

Ford stood on the hill overlooking one of golf's most historic, demanding second shots—down into the valley, over a wide but narrow stream that fronts a slick green that steeply slopes from back to front. It was here, in the shadow of Ford's ball, where Gene Sarazen made a name for the Masters, golf, and himself by launching his famous double eagle in 1935. This is also where Seve Ballesteros would smother-hook a 4-iron approach shot into the hazard, clearing the way for Jack Nicklaus to don a sixth green jacket in 1986.

That is enough perspective to wreck the nerves, but here stood thirty-four-year-old Douglas Michael Ford, native New Yorker, former pool shark, 1955 PGA Championship winner, remembering yesterday with just three and a half holes remaining in the 1957 Masters. He grew up in New York City in the shadow of the Polo Grounds, the New York Giants' home baseball field, and developed an affection for pool-hall billiards as a youngster, racking up as many as twenty-five to thirty-five consecutive shots in "straight" pool. His grandfather was an Italian immigrant railroad man with the name Fortunato, which Doug's father, a golf pro, changed to Ford.

Also, understand that Ford was considered somewhat of a hothead in the day. Ford was known to openly criticize the slower-paced players and once berated the Professional Golfers Association of America authorities to penalize a player who held back his brisk pace of play. In 1955, Ford once even questioned whether women in the gallery should be allowed to wear shorts to tournaments because he found them "distracting."

So, you would have to believe that any negative thoughts either from the previous day or about the fifteenth hole in general could erode the confidence of Doug Ford.

It was from this exact spot in Saturday's third round of the 1957 Masters where Ford had watched in horror as his 3-wood second shot flew to the bank on the other side, stopped in its pitch mark, and slowly rolled back into the hazard. Ford gallantly took off his shoes and socks, rolled up his pants legs, trudged in to blast out his ball in a shower of muddy creek water, and salvaged a bogey. Good-bye Yankee, most thought.

Doug Ford, the 1957 Masters champion, chips to a green on the way to his victory as his caddie George "Fireball" Franklin *(left)* and the gallery watch. Ford and Franklin had a disagreement on the fifteenth fairway in Sunday's final round. (© *Augusta Chronicle*)

Ford trailed the third-round leader, West Virginia's Sam Snead, by three strokes.

"When I got to the clubhouse after that round, a couple of old-time pros said if I got a chance at fifteen tomorrow, lay up," Ford said. Adding another negative thought, it was on this back nine in 1956 where Ford was tied with Jackie Burke and "blew up" to finish five strokes behind Burke, the eventual champion.

Twenty-four hours after his wet fifteenth on Saturday, Ford reached the exact same position, staring some 230 yards into the distance on the 500-yard par 5. He had played brilliantly—4-under par through fourteen holes—to catch and pass Slammin' Sammy, who was one stroke back after consecutive bogeys early on the back nine.

Enter one George "Fireball" Franklin, an Atlantan who was first assigned to caddie for Ford in his 1952 Masters debut.

"I like to carry sticks for a fast golfer," Fireball said. "When you go fast you got no time to think of anything but the next shot. But when you play with a slow one ... well, my mind wanders. First thing you know I'm thinking about my gal uptown, or bad whiskey, or something like that."

As Ford tried to quickly forget about Saturday, Fireball would not let him. Ford was noted for his rapid-fire pace of play and a quick, flat golf swing that he characterized as that of a "gorilla golfer." His self-confidence was legendary also. In the weeks leading up to the 1957 Masters, *Golf World* magazine polled 150 golfers to predict the Masters winner; Ford was the only one who picked himself. Ford was reaching to select the 3-wood when Fireball spoke up.

"Use your 4-iron," Fireball shot out. "Gonna cost me $100 if you go in the water."

Ford went ahead with his attempt to unsheathe his 3-wood. Fireball, acting the part of a good banker, was persistent. Ford grasped again. Fireball moved the bag a bit, away from Ford's reach. The gallery noticed the goings-on and a murmur of nervous laughter came up.

Finally, Ford took charge.

"Snead is right behind us and he'll easily be able to reach

this green in two," Ford said forcefully. "I'm no good at playing safe. Besides, they don't remember you here unless you go for it and win."

With that, Fireball let his guard down. Ford drew the 3-wood and ripped at his second shot. The ball took a low trajectory, barely cleared the hazard, and, instead of retreating as it had done on Saturday, hopped up on the green. Ford, a deft putter, easily two-putted from forty feet for birdie.

Ford punctuated his victory with a hole-out birdie from a bunker on the eighteenth hole, a shot that completed a 6-under-par 66, the best final-round Masters score to date. It was also one of only three Masters bogey-free final rounds to date. Ford tossed his sand wedge skyward and rejoiced at what would be a three-stroke victory over Snead. As luck would have it, the CBS cameras did not catch the finale, coming on the air just after Ford completed his round.

But as Ford signed his scorecard and awaited the final pairings, Fireball was still fuming at the give and take on fifteen.

"It worked this year," Fireball said. "But it ain't gonna work next, I'm telling ya. Man 4-under par shoulda played it safe."

Fireball would continue to tote for Ford through the mid-1960s. Ford described him as a "steady caddie."

"We got along real well," Ford said in 2000. "He knew the course and he knew me."

True to Fireball's steadfastness, Ford has been the Masters' man of one mind, a champion of the past with a gruff exterior and eternal pride in his accomplishments. He and other veteran Masters winners age sixty and above received a letter from Augusta National Chairman Hootie Johnson in 2001 asking them not to play any longer, a policy which was later rescinded but got its point across to the likes of Ford. Ford had played in a record forty-nine Masters (tied with Arnold Palmer entering 2004). Critics chirped up every year, questioning his place among golf's elite. Here was a man in his late seventies who had not played the Champions Tour in nearly a decade, had not broken 80 in the Masters since 1990, had not made the cut in a Masters since 1971 and often called it a tournament after eighteen holes or even just nine or less.

Many a prying media member would monotonously ask: Why play?

"Because I won the damn tournament," Ford said with a scowl on his face.

Somewhere, finally, Fireball was smiling.

Arnie and Iron Man:
The Corporation

For Arnold Palmer, it was all about being a flamboyant player and wearing his heart on his sleeve. Go for broke, show emotion, and capture the crowd with good looks and a quick smile. If anyone could take the game of golf on his shoulders and rocket the sport to a higher echelon in the early days of televised golf of the late 1950s, it was the man everyone simply called Arnie.

Arnie did not need someone to share the stage or direct his playing path. He simply needed an understanding compatriot, a caddie who knew how to press Arnie's buttons, a man who could walk quietly by his side and just mutter a few words of encouragement or, better yet, instill discipline when the time came.

That man was Nathaniel Avery, an Augustan who was born to golf and claimed the most endearing nickname in the caddie yard, "Iron Man." It was a nickname that fit the bill for the caddie to a man with steel-town roots and the hard-working, go-for-broke persona of Arnold Palmer from Latrobe, Pennsylvania. It became a partnership shared in four Masters titles.

Described by Will Grimsley of the Associated Press as "a lean rope of a man, with just a trace of a mustache and a goatee, standing about 6-foot, 155 pounds," Avery was the perfect balance for Palmer. He had a loping stride, was quiet, usually

Arnold Palmer watches a shot with caddie Nathaniel "Iron Man" Avery at his side in 1960. Iron Man's remark, "Mr Palmer, are we chokin'?" in the 1960 tournament inspired Palmer to birdie the final two holes and win his second Masters by one stroke. (© Historic Golf Photos/ Ron Watts Collection)

expressionless on the golf course (called "sad-faced" in one early 1960's newspaper account), and could be found many times resting his haunches on Palmer's bag or sprawled casually on his side, head propped up by a hand, as Palmer putted. "He was rather quiet and laid back," Palmer says today. When Arnie birdied the last two holes in 1960 to capture his second Masters title, there was Iron Man sitting on the bag on the right side of the eighteenth green as Arnie jumped up and down and the entire gallery responded. The emotion was usually left to Arnie, whom Iron Man just simply called "Par."

Born in 1939, Nathaniel was the youngest of eight children, four boys and four girls. His oldest brother, "Big Henry," was the longtime caddie master at Augusta Country Club and the man largely responsible for training young caddies and giving many of them their nicknames when they "graduated" to work north of Rae's Creek at Augusta National. Big Henry earned his nickname because of his six-feet-four, 300-pound build and booming voice, quite a contrast to the smaller, thinner Nathaniel.

Another brother, Horace, was the assistant caddie master at Augusta National. A third brother, Willie, also became an Augusta National caddie. Nathaniel's future brother-in-law, Willie "Pappy" Stokes, married his sister Odella. Pappy was a five-time Masters winner as a caddie, mentor to the caddies from the 1950s to 1970s, and claimed by many as the best to ever step foot on Augusta National.

Decades later, a great nephew, William, would become a star guard in basketball at Duke University. He was a first-round draft pick of the NBA's Minnesota Timberwolves, where he played for three years as a backup guard before playing in Europe in 2002–2003. William had met or exceeded the fame of his great uncle. A public, outdoor basketball court located approximately one mile from Augusta National, around the corner off Berckmans Road, on Wheeler Road at Big Oak Park, bears the names of William and Ricky Moore, former Augusta National caddie Buck's son. William and Ricky formed a deadly backcourt duo to lead nearby Westside High School to the 1995 Georgia Class AAA state basketball title, losing only one game all season. William's No. 1–ranked Duke team and Moore's Connecticut Huskies faced off in the 1999 NCAA Championship game in St. Petersburg, Florida, with the Huskies prevailing.

It was before the family's fame that Nathaniel naturally hung out in the caddie yard in the early 1950s. As a 115-pound kid, Nathaniel boasted that he could carry the heaviest bag of the day's rounds at either Augusta Country Club or Augusta National and come back for more. That was the first time, he said in a mid-1960s interview, that someone jokingly called him Iron Man.

Another tale claims that Iron Man was missing a couple fingertips after some sort of accident. One theory, told by veteran Augusta National caddie Joe Collins, claims that Iron Man, evidently under the influence of alcohol, once tried to cut open a golf ball with an ax and lopped some fingertips off in the process. Another states that he suffered the injury by holding an exploding firecracker. Yet another account relates that wounds suffered in a knife fight did not bleed.

Whatever the origin, the question was inevitably asked: "What do you think, you're an Iron Man or something?"

Caddying would be Nathaniel's future, for sure, but playing was his first love. By the mid-1950s, a teenaged Nathaniel was able to shoot sub-par golf. In those days, caddies could occasionally play both Augusta National and Augusta Country Club at specified times, and Nathaniel's best scores were an even-par 72 at Augusta National and 68 at Augusta Country Club. In 1961, he shot a final-round 70 at an open amateur tournament in New York and then made his way back to lug Arnie's bag in the Masters. He won the Augusta National caddie tournament, held in late spring before the course closed for the summer, at least four times.

"With the right opportunity, he could have played the (PGA) Tour," said Freddie Bennett, the former Augusta National caddie master.

But the world of the 1950s was not ready for a black man to make his way as a player. That, and Arnold Palmer came on the scene.

It was 1955 when Palmer first came to the Masters, invited as the reigning U.S. Amateur champion. Arnie and his wife, Winnie, towed their twenty-six-foot trailer into Augusta and steered it into a trailer park off Gordon Highway for tournament week. Hot-shot young players like Ken Venturi, Mike Souchak, and Gene Littler drew most of the attention from the press and the caddies. Caddie assignments were made either by request of the players, reference from the caddie master, or simply by assignment.

"The caddie master came down to the lot and said, 'If you take this bag, you got to keep it.' I said, 'I'll keep it,' " Iron Man said. "Even though Ken Venturi was the heat, I'll keep it."

For fourteen years, Nathaniel Avery was Palmer's right-hand man at Augusta National. He was the rare caddie who was

Arnold Palmer *(right)* and caddie Nathaniel "Iron Man" Avery react to a missed eagle putt on the par-5 thirteenth hole during the final round of the 1964 Masters. Palmer three-putted for par but went on to become the first man to win four Masters titles. The 1964 victory was Palmer's last Masters title. (© Historic Golf Photos/Ron Watts Collection)

interviewed by the press, calling the partnership "a corporation, a team." Iron Man often responded with down-home insight about golf's new superstar. He even painted the long-lasting image of Arnie and his patented charging style.

"He just hitch his trousers, jerk on his glove, starts walking fast and says, 'The game is on,' " Iron Man said in the 1960s. "When Mr. Arnold do that, everybody better watch out. He's gonna stampede anything in his way."

On the player-caddie relationship: "Anybody who can't get along with Mr. Arnold can't get along with anybody. I should know. I been almost in his pocket on every hole.

"Sometime he go with my advice—and it better be right. If I mis-club him, he don't chastise me. He just look a little mean, and I feel like going through the ground. But he is a great man."

On Palmer playing his best golf when the tournament began: "Par hittin' the ball just as good as ever, but he's puttin' worse than I've ever seen him putt in a long time.... He ain't too worried, though, and I ain't either. When they ring the bell, he'll be there. He lays one up for birdie, he'll make it."

On Palmer's ability to overcome adversity, rallying from a double bogey in the final round in 1962 to force a Monday play-off, where he beat Dow Finsterwald and Gary Player: "He just look up in the sky like he is wishing for some miracle to come down. And the miracle come down—like somebody was answering him."

Arnie's first Masters win in 1958 also evoked humor.

Entering the final round tied for the lead with Sam Snead at 5-under par, word was passed down by Augusta National chairman and cofounder Clifford Roberts to all players near the lead that a Sunday victory could possibly mean an invitation for a Monday tee time with the most famous American golfer, Dwight D. Eisenhower, the sitting president of the United States and a member of Augusta National. Eisenhower's passion for golf, paired beginning in the late 1950s with Palmer's rise to fame, would bring great new exposure to the game.

"If you couple the pressure of contending at the Masters with the thought that you might play golf with the president of the United States the next day, you can imagine what I went through the final eighteen holes that day," Palmer said.

The tension was heightened early in the back nine when Palmer and an ornery rules official on the twelfth hole butted heads. Arnie's tee shot on the par-3 hole embedded in rain-soaked, soft turf behind the green, just a few feet below a bunker. Arnie studied his lie and upcoming second shot and asked for relief from the wet area. The rules official denied his request. According to legendary golf writer Herbert Warren Wind's account, there was "an animated and protracted dis-

Ken Venturi *(left)* and Arnold Palmer *(right)* discuss a ruling decision during the final round of the 1958 Masters with (in cart) Augusta National and Masters cofounders Bobby Jones and Clifford Roberts. Palmer learned from Jones during this conversation that he was given a par on the twelfth hole, instead of a double bogey, on the fifteenth hole. (© *Augusta Chronicle*)

cussion" between Palmer and the rules official. With his dander up, Palmer still had enough patience to think through the process. He slopped the ball out and made a double bogey. However, he then played a provisional ball and got up and down for par. It was in question whether Palmer retained a one-stroke lead over playing partner Venturi or fell one behind the San Francisco amateur. The final verdict was yet to come.

Arnie took care of some of that indecision on the next shots at the dogleg left, par-5 thirteenth. He slashed a 250-yard drive around the corner, then a choked-down 3-wood onto the green eighteen feet to the left and above the hole and rolled in the eagle putt. Two holes later, Bobby Jones came out to officially inform them that Palmer's par on the twelfth hole stood. Arnie beat Doug Ford and Fred Hawkins by one stroke to capture his first major championship.

The hysteria that resulted from the victory caused nearly as much confusion among the Palmer family.

"I told Winnie right away that I was going to play golf with the president the next day," Palmer recalled. "And in the same sentence, I asked Winnie to write Iron Man a check. It was normal to give a sizable check to the caddie of the player who wins the Masters."

Arnie asked Winnie, who doubled as his traveling secretary and bookkeeper in those early days, to pay Iron Man $1,400. An overjoyed gallery and friends gathered to give their congratulations. Arnie and Iron Man evidently were also engrossed in a debate that had something to do with a set of clubs as Winnie wrote out the check. Finally, the Palmers were able to break away from Augusta National as a group of friends and club representatives from Wilson Sporting Goods treated the winning couple to dinner and drinks in downtown Augusta at the Town Tavern, the traditional restaurant and watering hole for the Masters participants. But before they could complete the meal, an urgent call came from officials at Augusta National.

Winnie had written a check for $14,000, more than the $11,250 first prize, and Iron Man was attempting to cash it at the clubhouse. Augusta National officials immediately contacted the Town Tavern to question the exorbitant fee. The matter was resolved, with an extra zero being eliminated from the check. Iron Man was told to pick up the new check at the Richmond Hotel, the Broad Street hotel where many of the players stayed during the tournament.

The date with Ike was delayed until after Arnie's 1960 win at the Masters, but Iron Man had become a fixture. In June 1960, *Sport* magazine chronicled a first-person account by Iron Man of what it was like to carry Palmer's clubs. He was one of the first Masters caddies to be interviewed by the press, indeed a rarity in those days when caddies were often perceived as nothing more than a hired hand, much less a good subject for an interview.

Most importantly, Arnie remembers Iron Man in 1960 on his way to winning his second Masters title. Chain-smoking L&M cigarettes and swigging Coca-Colas on the back nine to fight nervousness, Palmer was throwing away shots left and right. He trailed by one stroke entering the back nine, failed to birdie the short par-5 thirteenth, and saw the tournament slipping away. By the time Arnie reached No. 14, Venturi had already posted a 5-under-par 283 total. Arnie needed a birdie coming home to tie. A poor pitch on his third shot from beside the par-5 fifteenth green blew another birdie chance and infuriated Arnie. He tossed his wedge at Iron Man, who was standing nearby at Palmer's bag.

The stare he got back was startling.

"Mr. Palmer," Iron Man said in his usual low-pitched growl. "Are we chokin'?"

The query perked Palmer up. He might not win, but nobody accuses Arnie of being gutless. On the par-3 sixteenth, a bold long birdie putt rattled the flag and he was left with a tap-in for par. Faced with a birdie-birdie finish to win, Arnie drilled a thirty-five-footer on the seventeenth to tie Venturi, and then sank a five-footer on the closing hole to win his second Masters. Iron Man had delivered his message.

"His scowl (on the fifteenth hole) was eerily reminiscent of the disapproving glare Pap (father Deacon) used to give me as a kid whenever I threw a club or failed to keep my mind on the job," Palmer wrote in his 1999 biography, *A Golfer's Life*.

"Iron Man wasn't the greatest caddie. I'd be less than honest if I said he was. His distances were often inaccurate, and I relied, instead, on my own calculations and the knowledge of the course to get around Augusta. But his understanding of what made me tick was perhaps instinctive and definitely profound. I stared back at him and realized he was right—I was foolishly beating on myself instead of taking care of the business of playing the golf course."

Today, Palmer recounts that Iron Man "was a good Augusta caddie … he was solid and did his job."

If Iron Man was the steadying influence on the golf course, he was anything but that away from Augusta National. The fame he had gained from being Palmer's right-hand man transformed Iron Man into a man about town in Augusta's black community during the 1960s. With every one of Palmer's four victories, Iron Man went out and purchased a new, shiny Cadillac or Pontiac to transport him and the girlfriend of that particular day to the nearest crap game or nightclub.

"In my mind, he was the black sheep of the family," says Carl Jackson. "He was a real gambler, a ladies' man type of guy, not a family man. On weekends, you'd see him all over the area, gambling and shooting dice. He also visited the jailhouse a few times."

Henry Avery Jr., the son of Big Henry, remembers his uncle as "a freewheeler, but a nice guy."

"I looked up to him as a kid," Henry Jr. says. "That's the way we were led to believe. Every time he'd buy a new car, he'd come by and pick me up and take me for a ride. He'd let me think I was driving that car.

"He was just loving life. He loved the night life. It wasn't anything out of the ordinary; he just loved to party."

The partying took a toll on Iron Man and his prized cars from the outset. Late on Monday night following Palmer's first victory in 1958, it did not take long for Iron Man to dispose of the reissued (and downsized) check. Iron Man was cruising down Wheeler Road in a new Pontiac purchased just that afternoon, with a female acquaintance close by his side and a beverage in hand. The car veered off the side of the road and struck a tree near an elementary school. No serious injuries were reported, just a totaled vehicle and an Iron Man visit to University Hospital, where the medical staff soon discovered his identity and took pity on his quickly lost wages.

"Too bad you don't have anything left from caddying for the new Masters champion," one doctor remarked.

"Oh yes, I have, I got these thirty dollar shoes," Iron Man said as he grinned and proudly stuck one foot in the air from the hospital bed.

"The bark peeled off that tree where the car hit it and stayed off for years and years," Henry Jr. says. "People used to say that's where Iron Man left his mark. That mark stayed there till that tree died."

By the late 1960s, Arnie's reign as the King of the Masters was at its end. With a second-round 79 in the 1968 Masters, Palmer totaled 151 to miss the cut for the first time. He trudged through the round as Arnie's Army sat on its hands at the horror of the occasion. Palmer was invited by Roberts to stay around for lunch and a quick tour of the course in a golf cart for Saturday's third round, which he obliged, then took off in his jet, bound for home in Latrobe.

It was also to be the last time that Arnie and Iron Man shared the bag in the Masters. The talk was that Arnie had had enough of Iron Man staking a share of the credit for some of the successful run at Augusta National. "He was getting too big for his britches" was the word around the Augusta National caddie shack. Another report stated that a national magazine wished to do a story on Palmer and asked for Iron Man's input. His response: "How much you gonna pay me?" Winnie was standing nearby, overheard the pay request, and grew disgusted with Iron Man's attitude. Arnie was also famous for changing caddies on a whim. An Associated Press account in 1964 said that in the U.S. Open that year at Congressional Country Club in Washington, D.C., Palmer changed caddies three times before the tournament even started. But, most likely, Iron Man's caddying skills had been eroded by his off-course antics and failing health. Arnie simply said in 2003 that "(Iron Man) didn't show up the next year (1969)." Bennie Hatcher, still a regular caddie at Augusta National today, was hired to take Iron Man's place and carried Arnie's bag through 1977.

By the mid-1970s, Iron Man was a sad figure, hanging around the fringes of the tournament, trying to catch any odd job that came his way. Caddying was out of the question for a man who was still only in his mid-thirties.

"I ain't got nothing now," Iron Man said in 1974. "I've had no action since 1971. I got a job this year carrying a photographer's equipment. Then they fired me. Said I was too slow."

Still, there was the confident attitude that said this man believed he could still tote with the best of them.

"But no man knows this course like me," Iron Man said. "I know every tree, every blade of grass, every break of the greens. Arnie will be lucky to make the cut. He's having his problems. He'll never make a comeback until he gets me back. You just wait and see."

True to Iron Man's prediction, Palmer never contended again after the breakup. His best finish was a tie for eleventh in 1974.

Iron Man's name was fading from the headlines. But by the mid-1970s, the Avery family became involved in a dispute *against* Augusta National.

On the afternoon of Tuesday, October 18, 1976, three young black boys were shot at Augusta National after they entered the grounds to fish in Rae's Creek near the twelfth green. Charles Avery, age nineteen, suffered the worst damage, listed as serious wounds by the hospital, to the upper right side and chest area. Charles' brother, Robert, age twelve, was wounded in the upper right arm and right thighbone area. A third injured person, Justin Jackson, age nineteen, was wounded in the right leg. All three were admitted to University Hospital. Charles and Robert were the sons of "Big Henry" Avery, the Augusta Country Club caddie master, and the nephews to Horace and Iron Man.

Phil Wahl, the general manager of Augusta National, said that the shooting was an accident. A group of boys was spotted on the grounds in mid-afternoon by nurseryman Rogers Bennett, who said one of the boys was carrying a small shotgun, probably used to ward off snakes, which can be found most often in the Rae's Creek tributary which flows left of the thirteenth fairway. The boys left when Bennett asked them to, but they returned to the Rae's Creek area a short time later, apparently without the gun. Bennett summoned security guard Charles Young when he spotted them on the property. The club had just opened for the season and interlopers were not allowed. Armed with a 12-gauge pump-action shotgun, Young accompanied Bennett down to Amen Corner. When the boys saw the men approaching, they ran.

"The guard was in the act of loading his shotgun with the thought of firing over the heads of the boys as a means of causing them to stop and identify themselves," Wahl said in the October 19, 1976 *Augusta Chronicle.* "Unfortunately, the gun was discharged (from about fifty yards away), quite by accident, according to the club guard (and they were struck with magnum buckshot)."

The Richmond County Sheriff's Department began an investigation. All of the boys were released from the hospital shortly thereafter. However, the community was stunned. Just eighteen months before, Lee Elder had become the first black man to play in the Masters. Then this occurred, oddly enough to family members of well-known, longtime members of the Augusta National/Augusta Country Club golf community.

By May 1977, the three wounded boys began a series of legal proceedings. Robert Avery, through his father "Big Henry," filed an $11 million damage complaint in Richmond County Superior Court against Augusta National, stating that Robert suffered "permanent disfigurement and disability." More alarming was the conclusion of the filing, which stated, "Augusta National Inc. deliberately pursues a policy of racism in membership, employment, ticket sales and other matters, and that Young's actions occurred because the plaintiff and his companions are black." Charles Avery and Justin Jackson followed soon after with charges of damages for their injuries.

By June, Augusta National attorney William C. Calhoun argued that the shooting was an accident and also strongly asked the court to delete the portion of the suit referring to racism, partly because it might "prejudice the minds of prospective black jurors." The boys returned a suit also charging the maker of Young's shotgun, High Standard Sporting Firearms, which was claimed by Augusta National to be defective. Robert's initial $11 million suit was dropped, and another began, this time filed by his mother. The three boys' final suits, filed separately in 1978, eventually totaled $6 million in damage requests.

The cases dragged on until the week after the 1979 Masters when the U.S. District Court in Augusta was scheduled to hold jury trials. Juries were selected for two of the cases. Three days after Fuzzy Zoeller won the Masters on his first attempt and two and a half years after the shooting incident, attorneys for Augusta National and the firearms manufacturer, High Standard Sporting Firearms, met with the plaintiffs for two hours in the judge's quarters and settled for an undisclosed sum with the three boys. It was later revealed that the settlement was $15,000.00 apiece, according to a former Augusta National caddie.

Nevertheless, a bitter taste had been left in the mouths of the Avery family.

Iron Man's name was not mentioned in connection with the legal tug of war. That was probably for the best, since his caddying life was nearly at its end. He worked briefly for Calvin Peete in the early 1980s, but was only a shadow of his former self. The hard life had caught up with him.

"He really regressed," Jackson says. "He didn't take care of himself at all. He got senile, in my opinion. I caddied in the same group with him one time about then at Augusta National and he had the bag of a guest of one of the members for the weekend.

"The man studied a shot on one hole and asked, 'How far

have we got?' Iron Man just sort of stared at him and then blurted out, 'About a mile.' The man's face turned red; he was really offended. When the round was over, he let Iron Man go, fired him right there. Iron Man was a sick man."

Henry Jr. says the cause of Iron Man's death at age forty-seven on May 6, 1985 was liver disease caused by alcohol abuse. He had also developed tuberculosis a few years before, according to Jariah Beard, thereby accelerating his ailment by drinking too much.

The *Augusta Chronicle* carried a simple sixty-one-word obituary on May 7, 1985. It gave his nickname, "Iron Man," and stated that he was a member of Elim Baptist Church, but listed no occupation or tie-in to the Masters or Palmer. He never married or had children. There would be no other stories or reminiscence about his glory days as a caddie. Nathaniel E. Avery died a broken man with what some deemed a glorious past.

A simple funeral was held at Dent's Undertaking Establishment. He is buried in the expansive Southview Cemetery in downtown Augusta near the intersection of Martin Luther King Jr. Boulevard and Fifteenth Street. There is no headstone or marker to identify his final resting place, just a map and listing in the cemetery office which points out the location as "Grave No. 3, Lot No. 12, Section G."

"He didn't die with any celebrity status," says Henry Jr., who served as a pallbearer at his uncle's funeral. "He was just a caddie. I mean, I'm proud of him, doing what he did. He was famous. But just remember, he was just a caddie."

Player's Triumphant Duo

Gary Player arrived at the 1978 Masters Tournament with two green jackets in his closet and the career Grand Slam on his resume. He had earned a spot in the World Golf Hall of Fame and was already revered as one of the game's foremost international ambassadors.

Still, his caddie felt comfortable enough with their relationship to confide in the forty-two-year-old dynamo. Eddie McCoy wanted to inspire his boss, and make a big payday in the process.

"You gotta win this tournament, man," McCoy lamented as the tournament began. "I'm in trouble and I need a new house. We gotta win."

The house was on order when Player stormed through the final round. He birdied seven of the final ten holes, including a downhill fifteen-footer on the eighteenth hole, to come from seven strokes back with a final-round 64 and win the Masters, at that time becoming the oldest champion in tournament history. Player and McCoy walked onto the eighteenth green arm in arm with huge smiles on their faces.

"I don't know what kind of trouble Eddie was in, but when I came from seven strokes back on Sunday, you've never seen a man as happy as Eddie was," Player says. "There's a picture taken just after I holed the putt on eighteen. In it, you see Eddie flying toward me like Batman, from the left of the green, with an expression on his face as though he'd just won the lottery."

Eddie McCoy *(left)* and Gary Player study the line of a putt during the 1977 Masters. Player and McCoy worked together at the Masters on and off through 1992. (Photograph by Lee Downing, © *Augusta Chronicle*)

The pressure of a tight Sunday at the Masters was enough for anyone. But Player's Masters performances are full of stress, both on and off the course. He won three titles with two different caddies, Ernest Nipper (1961) and McCoy (1974 and 1978), and almost a fourth time with another caddie.

Begin with 1961. Player was far from the fan favorite, not only because he was not an American but also because Arnold Palmer was charging toward a third green jacket. That is when the green-side bunkers on the eighteenth hole made the difference. Palmer, holding a one-stroke lead over Player in the final pairing, made double bogey from the right greenside bunker. Player had gotten up and down for par from the same place just a few minutes earlier to get a chance to make a game of it.

Perhaps what kept Player in the race that week was his caddie Ernest Nipper. Nipper was known as a great player who stalked the course as if he was trying to win the tournament himself. Right away, he established some credibility with Player.

"We were playing the fourth hole, a par 3, in the first round," Player says. "I had a putt of about fifteen feet left of the hole, going up to the hole. I thought I had to hit it to the left edge. Most of the time, I read all my putts. But this putt confused me. So I asked Nipper. He said, 'Right edge,' so emphatically. I wasn't so sure of that.

"All he said was, 'Gary, if it doesn't break to the left, you don't have to pay me this week.' Sure enough, the putt broke left into the hole. That made the difference in my confidence all week. I had somebody with me who could really help."

Player's relationship with Nipper continued through the 1960s, but it ended in bizarre fashion at the 1970 Masters.

Protesters of apartheid, South Africa's racially exclusive policy, were focusing on Player as a high-profile representative of South Africa. Even though Player was opposed to this type of government, he was duly associated with the movement. His usual all-black garb drew the attention of fans and political activists. Player would not criticize the South African government for fear of endangering friends and relatives back home.

The protests got ugly during the 1969 PGA Championship at NCR Country Club in Dayton, Ohio. During the third round, protesters from the Dayton Organization, a coalition representing such groups as the Students for a Democratic Society and the Southern Christian Leadership Conference, broke through the gallery ropes and charged onto the tenth green. A bearded, young white man exchanged words with Player. A few other protesters approached Jack Nicklaus, Player's playing partner, as the Golden Bear was lining up a putt, but Jack pulled back his putter in defense just as one of the protesters picked up his ball. Player was jostled as security forces arrested the demonstrators. Later in the round, a 278-page PGA Championship program, water, and a golf ball were tossed at Player in separate incidents, with security rushing to apprehend the demonstrators. Through it all, Player somehow focused and finished second to Raymond Floyd on Sunday.

Two years later, during the 1971 U.S. Open at Merion, Player would be heckled by a couple of black spectators in the

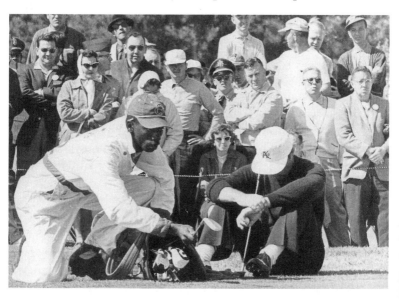

Ernest Nipper reads a putt for Gary Player who rests nearby in 1961, Player's first Masters title. Nipper was nicknamed "Snipes" because of his ability to read greens. (© *Augusta Chronicle*)

first round and had to be accompanied by a uniformed police officer for the remainder of the tournament.

So you could picture the tension around Gary Player during these trying times. Here was a small, unbelievably physically fit man who could be billed the Jack La Lanne of golf. Player stayed in the condition of a lightweight boxer by doing push-ups and sit-ups and even tried weight lifting, long considered a no-no for golfers, long before the current craze of hitting the gym before and after a round of golf. Player also traditionally wore black to bring attention to his golf game, differing distinctly in dress from the usually placid grays and whites of 1960s golf fashion. He wore black because his father told him to differentiate himself from the norm. Players' favorite cowboy, actor Richard Boone as Paladin in the 1950s Western TV series *Have Gun, Will Travel,* wore an all-black getup. Player also silently figured that by wearing the dark color in the heat he could draw power from the sun.

But it was also ironic that Player regularly had a black caddie, both at the Masters, which was of course mandatory, and during regular play elsewhere in the world. Alfred "Rabbit" Dyer, a tall, gangly black man, was Player's right-hand man just about everywhere but the Masters. Rabbit wore colorful clothing, outlandish hats, and dark glasses and was an intimidating presence beside the much-shorter Player.

By the middle of 1971, Player was breaking new ground for his stance on racial efforts. In June 1971, Player offered Lee Elder, the top black American golfer of the day, an invitation to visit South Africa and play in the South African PGA Championship. After some deliberation about the specifics of the visit, Elder accepted and played in the event that December, opening the doors for many South African black golfers to participate in their national tournaments. The participation would lead Player to lobby former Masters champions in early 1972 to issue an invitation to Elder as the first black Masters invitee. Player found out from 1959 Masters champion Art Wall that the former champions' invite, long a last-ditch method to get a shunned golfer into the Masters field, had been canceled a few years prior. Player pulled for Elder to win a PGA Tour event and earn a Masters spot (he did three years later in 1975) and said to the Associated Press in March 1972 that "Charlie Sifford would have been in the Masters years ago had qualifications been as they are today."

Still, Player's ties to his homeland were placed in the spotlight as the 1970s began.

Security for Player was tightened for the 1970 season. A trench-coated security guard hovered around Player during the PGA Tour stop at Doral Resort and Spa early in the year, just over a month before the Masters. But there were no incidents.

Once the Tour came to Augusta National that spring, the stories ratcheted back up again. There was talk of more intense protests. First, Player met with Masters officials behind closed doors a couple times, once after shooting a 67 in Monday's practice round.

Gary Player and his caddie Ernest Nipper *(left)* prepare to play during the early 1960s. Player was paired with Chi Chi Rodriguez, who is lighting a cigar at the right. (© *Augusta Chronicle.*)

"I have no comment," Player said when he emerged from the meeting in the clubhouse. "I think it would be better if this whole thing were dropped. I am not mad at anybody. I love everybody regardless of race or religion."

That same day, Nipper opted to drop off Player's bag for fear that his life was in danger, switching to Chi Chi Rodriguez. Another caddie said that Nipper had been warned by a militant activist group not to work for Player during the Masters. For years, Nipper had met Player in Florida during the weeks preceding the Masters to prepare for the first major championship of the year. Without his crutch, Player leaned on a young, inexperienced Carl Jackson.

"The club officials didn't tell me too much about what was going on," Jackson said. "I was twenty-one or twenty-two and I wasn't paying too much attention to the newspaper accounts. Rumor was that Nipper got some death threats and that really scared him. Pretty soon, I started to pick up on things. We had our own Secret Service-like guy walking by my side, especially during the practice rounds. He told me that even when I didn't see him he would be there. We went through the whole tournament like that."

But it was a successful relationship, particularly when Jackson gained Player's trust. Despite the presence of five plain-clothes officers and three uniformed Pinkerton guards at one time, Player was a strong contender. At first, Player told Jackson that he would club himself and read his own putts. After Jackson volunteered some suggestions in the practice round, Player gave in and utilized Jackson's input during the tournament. A bogey on the seventy-second hole kept Player out of the Billy Casper–Gene Littler play-off.

Nipper would never caddie in the Masters again after that year, choosing to move to New York, where he had family, and enter private business.

That brought on McCoy, as Jackson was assigned Charlie Coe the next year. The relationship with McCoy lasted for more than twenty years, until 1992, with McCoy toting some for Player on the Senior PGA Tour. When Rabbit Dyer made his only two trips to work for Player at Augusta National in the early 1990s, Player made sure that McCoy had a bag, working for David Frost, a young South African star. McCoy worked for Frost through 1994.

The Player-McCoy duo took their first title in 1974, thanks to one of Player's greatest shots ever. Leading by one stroke as they walked to Player's tee shot on the par-4 seventeenth, the pre-shot thoughts were not good. The straight-away par-4 hole with the difficult green had always been a thorn in Player's side.

"Eddie, in all the years I've played here, I don't think I've hit this green six times," Player remarked as they stared at the approach shot from just under 150 yards.

Faced with a 9-iron approach shot to the usual final-round, right-side pin placement, Player hit his shot and almost immediately put the club back in the bag and began to walk toward the green.

"No, I didn't look," Player said. "I asked Eddie, 'Do you think we're going to putt this one?'"

He almost did not have to, as the ball stopped within inches of the cup on the way to his second Masters title.

Player's reliance on his caddies in his Masters victories transcended the controversial issues he confronted during the socially active 1960s and 1970s.

"The caddies in the U. S. Open don't mean much," Player said in 1974. "They usually give you a young boy so you won't ask him for information. The British Open is about the same thing. In the PGA, you also get young caddies.

"But in this tournament, the majority of the caddies live here. Eddie lives here and knows the greens well. Caddies in the Masters play a more important role than any major tournament."

Gary Player can attest to that.

Cricket Covers for Coody

In every Masters Tournament victory, there is a key swing thought, a lucky charm or a moment that puts the player at ease, a simple antidote to get rid of the jitters or convince the player that this is his week.

For Charles Coody, the 1971 Masters brought the usual assortment of superstitions: his favorite sweet potato biscuits, a pair of lucky old green trousers, and an English half-penny that his eight-year-old daughter had given him to mark his ball. But more than anything, the path to the green jacket was paved by one Walter Pritchett, better known in caddie circles as Cricket.

Cricket worked occasionally for Coody at other events on the PGA Tour and was his caddie for the 1969 Masters when they almost won. But Coody, one stroke ahead with three holes to play that year, bogeyed in to allow George Archer to sneak in. Coody placed in a tie for fifth, two strokes back.

Cricket did not come back to Augusta National in 1970. He deferred for a steady job as a bus driver in his hometown of Atlanta. Coody started out with another caddie in 1971, but that caddie and Coody did not mesh.

"After a practice round on Sunday, I was walking through the parking lot and there was Cricket," Coody remembers. "He had gotten off from his bus-driving job in Atlanta and was just looking for a bag. So, since they assigned caddies, I had to go down to the tournament office and really discuss the situation. I eventually convinced them to let Cricket work for me."

The everyday Augusta National caddies did not care too much for an "outsider," albeit a former Augusta National regular, moving in on their turf for this one week. However, Coody wanted his lucky charm.

Coody surprised many by taking the first-round lead with a 6-under-par 66. Nobody was more shocked than Cricket come the third round.

As the duo walked up the par-5 eighth fairway on Saturday, the possibility of a tense weekend loomed. Coody was in

Charles Coody (*left*), the 1971 Masters champion, with his caddie Walter "Cricket" Pritchett. Cricket wore the towel under his cap to disguise himself when the CBS-TV cameras televised the final rounds of the tournament. Cricket skipped out on his job as a bus driver in Atlanta to caddie, telling his boss he needed to visit his sick grandmother in Houston. (© *Augusta Chronicle*)

contention, vying with Jack Nicklaus and Johnny Miller for the lead. But Cricket had other things on his mind.

"What time does the TV coverage start, Mr. Coody?" Cricket asked.

Coody seemingly did not hear.

"What hole does the TV start on?" Cricket came back again.

"Huh? I don't know," Coody muttered in his slow Texas drawl, then paused and looked at Cricket. "Why do you need to know that?"

There was another moment of silence as Cricket pondered Coody's question.

"Well, I told my boss in Atlanta that I needed time off to go visit my sick grandmother in Houston," Cricket said rather sheepishly.

"To be honest ... I didn't expect that you would play this well."

That broke the ice. Coody laughed all the way to the green and could not escape the thoughts of his caddie ducking his regular payday. As the back nine came during each weekend round, Coody was reminded again and again of Cricket's secret identity. Early in the back nine, Cricket would go into "his disguise," a small green and white Masters golf towel. He would take it off Coody's bag and drape it over his head under his Masters caddie cap to hide from the CBS-TV cameras. All you could see were his wire-rim glasses.

"It looked like I had some kind of Arabian caddying for me," Coody said. "It kept me from worrying about Nicklaus and Miller all the time."

Coody, tied with Nicklaus to begin the final round, fashioned a closing 2-under-par 70 to beat Nicklaus and Miller by two strokes for his only major championship. This time, with Cricket urging him on that three final pars would win the tournament, Coody birdied the par-3 sixteenth, the place where his trouble began two years before.

After the win, where Coody pocketed $25,000, Cricket was ready to get back behind the wheel of his bus on Monday morning in Atlanta. As he innocently strolled into the bus office, his supervisor peered over the counter with a big smile.

"You had a nice week, didn't you Cricket?" the supervisor said with a laugh. "Hope your grandmother didn't miss you."

Willie Peterson:
Jack's Right-Hand Man

The Character

Here are the words that they use to describe Willie Peterson, Jack Nicklaus' right-hand man in five of his six Masters victories: character, luck, hustle. These descriptions come from his peers in the Augusta National caddie ranks, his former boss, other players, his ex-wife, and his daughter.

Study these words carefully and you can quickly figure there could be a double meaning here. Did Peterson have character or was he simply a character? Was he a good-luck charm or just purely lucky to fall into a position of prominence among the famed Augusta National caddies? Did he prepare intensely to caddie, thereby earning a reputation as someone who hustled and worked extremely hard, or was he an out-and-out hustler, a man looking to make an extra buck in any way possible?

Peterson was truly a man of two faces, someone who could frustrate you with his penchant for being mischievous, yet at the same time, make you smile because of his bodacious attitude or good heart.

To a person, when you ask those associated with Peterson to assess his life and standing as a caddie, a smile creeps over their faces. Many shake their heads in memory of the tall tales about the man many simply called "Pete" or "Bro," the man who won more Masters titles (five) on one bag than anyone did.

But rest assured, Peterson was Nicklaus' lucky charm. He did not pull many clubs or read putts, but he was a vital cog in Jack's first five Masters titles.

"Willie was always a character, a good guy, I enjoyed having him work for me," Nicklaus says. "Outside of that, every time I came here he always said we (Nicklaus and company) had garnished his wages. Man, he was always in trouble, too, always in trouble. But he was fine. He was a great part of five of my six Masters titles."

Right away, you could see what made Peterson the most demonstrative caddie to ever loop in the Masters. Before play even started, there was Willie, full of himself, talking it up, pushing "Mr. Jack" as the out-and-out favorite, patting his man on the back to get him stoked for the round. To draw a parallel in another sport, Peterson was cornerman Drew "Bundini" Brown in the entourage of great heavyweight boxer Muhammad Ali, loud-mouthed, noticeable, and supremely confident.

Peterson's calling card on the course was flamboyance. There were the celebratory leaps, kicks, and fist pumps when Nicklaus was charging. He carried a towel over his shoulder on most occasions and would whip it off to sweep toward the ground matador-like when a promising putt was approaching the cup. From time to time, Willie would sprawl on the ground to read a putt. He chattered from shot to shot like an infielder goading the batter in baseball. He would occasionally salute the gallery when Nicklaus made a long putt.

Just about any picture you see of Nicklaus on the way to victory in 1963, 1965, 1966, 1972, or 1975 includes Willie nearby punching the air after a made putt, usually with the towel in hand. The cover of the April 17, 1972, issue of *Sports Illustrated* shows Willie confidently sticking his right arm straight up with the index finger extended and a cigarette tightly clinched between his pursed lips, just as Jack sinks another birdie putt. Willie is in the foreground, Jack in the background. Of the thirty-six *Sports Illustrated* covers featuring the Masters, Willie is the only Masters caddie to appear clearly in such a prominent position on the cover. Jimmy Dickinson, Nicklaus' longtime caddie in the British Open, and Bruce Edwards, Tom Watson's longtime sideman, are the only other caddies ever to prominently appear on any *Sports Illustrated* cover involving golf.

That he was the sidekick to the slow-paced, stoic, tunnel-visioned Nicklaus made for a diverse tandem. In contrast, Nicklaus' big rival of the 1960s, Arnold Palmer, was more like Peterson, outgoing and emotional on the course, and his caddie, Nathaniel "Iron Man" Avery, played the quiet, pensive role.

Nicklaus shared possibly his single most famous moment with Peterson. It was Sunday, April 13, 1975, and the duel was on late in the back nine. Tom Weiskopf and Johnny Miller were on Jack's heels in what has been billed as the greatest Masters battle ever. They came to the par-3 sixteenth hole with Weiskopf holding a one-stroke lead over Nicklaus after the tall sweet-swinger birdied the par-5 fifteenth. Nicklaus chose to wait on the sixteenth green so that the upcoming roar from Weiskopf's putt on No. 15 would not distract him.

"That is evil music ringing in Nicklaus' ears," said CBS announcer Ben Wright from his tower position on the fifteenth hole.

Weiskopf and Miller walked to the sixteenth tee, glaring across the pond as Nicklaus prepared for a long birdie putt. Play had been delayed when Nicklaus' playing partner Tom Watson hit two tee shots in the pond on No. 16. Wright and his British broadcasting partner Henry Longhurst were in the middle of one of the most historic calls in golf history.

Nicklaus faced a forty-foot birdie putt from the front left of the green, on the bottom tier, up through the long shadows of the tall pines late on Sunday afternoon, to a hole set on the top right shelf. It was a difficult two-putt at best. If the ball took the least bit of a turn to the left, it could filter down to the bottom left portion of the green, still forty or so feet away. Willie tended the pin as Nicklaus hunched down over his putt and studied the line. Finally, he gave the ball a hard smack with his George Low putter. As the ball rolled up the slope to

Jack Nicklaus *(back)* and caddie Willie Peterson study their next shot during the 1976 Masters Tournament. Peterson was on the bag for Nicklaus' first five Masters titles. (© *Augusta Chronicle*)

the second tier, Willie began motioning the ball home, and then started hopping up and down behind the hole as he pulled the flag and the ball fell in. Nicklaus, putter held high, charged around the lower tier of the green. The scene stirred legendary golf writer Dan Jenkins to write, "It made Nicklaus and his caddie, Willie Peterson, resemble Fred Astaire and Ginger Rogers."

"That has to be the greatest putt I ever saw in my life," Longhurst remarked on CBS from his tower behind the sixteenth green. Then there was a pause as the camera focused on the tee box. "And now Weiskopf will have to take it as he dished it out before."

Weiskopf, on the tee with the honor, looked as if he had seen a ghost, and yanked his tee shot left, took three to get down, and fell one stroke behind Nicklaus, who steered the victory home.

"I was always afraid sometime that Willie was gonna hit the ball with that towel because he got so excited," Nicklaus says. "He would be sitting there waving the ball in the hole and all I could think about was, 'Watch out!' "

"Willie was a little more animated than me. You never knew what Willie was gonna do. He was a piece of work."

Another routine depicts the sheer cockiness that made Peterson the perfect fit for Nicklaus, the most victorious major championship (eighteen professional, twenty including two U.S. Amateurs) and Masters golfer of all time.

Nicklaus would warm up on the driving range at Augusta National and then depart for the putting green to get his short game in gear before teeing off. Willie, with a sense that Nicklaus' game was primed, would leave the range and sprint down the hill toward the caddie shack, which was then stationed in the vicinity of where the main entrance corridor to the course is now located.

Willie would poke his head into where the caddies were lounging around, some shooting pool or playing cards, waiting for their respective tee times, and strike up a bold wager.

"Bet ya my man Mr. Jack doesn't make a bogey today," Willie would rattle off. "Anybody want some of that?"

As if a wildfire had hit the caddie house, Peterson had recorded bets all over the place. He would chime in with wagers for 69 or lower, nine-hole scores or high/low on how many birdies Jack would make that day.

Then he would continue his route to the other side of the clubhouse and catch up with Nicklaus at the putting green behind the first tee.

"Pappy, I hope you have a 68 and we have a red-hot 67," he told legendary caddie Willie "Pappy" Stokes in 1965 with the press corps listening. "If we get that 67, y'all can come back to talk to me and I'll tell you what's gonna happen the rest of the week."

"He was the only guy who made those types of bets," says Bennie Hatcher, a veteran caddie who began working at Au-

Jack Nicklaus *(left)* and caddie Willie Peterson celebrate in unison a made putt during Nicklaus' third title in 1966. Peterson was known for antics on the course, which included jumping, waving a towel, and saluting the gallery. It was rare for the usually stoic Nicklaus to display this much emotion. (© *Augusta Chronicle*)

gusta National in the early 1960s. "That was a foolish bet there to say his man would shoot in the 60s. He'd bet four or five people and bet them fifty dollars apiece. Naw, he never won. You don't make those kind of bets."

Willie may have lost a slew of wagers in the caddie house, but he loved every minute of being the center of attention. Maybe it is best to explain Willie Peterson by simply recalling how he developed this attitude.

Born in 1932, Willie was the second of five children in the Peterson household. The Petersons were not dirt poor—the reason some black kids in the day turned to caddying to earn a wage. Willie's parents, Willie Peterson Sr. and wife Josephine, were in the funeral home business. Haynes and Peterson Funeral Home was one of Augusta's first black-owned funeral homes, of which Willie's grandfather was cofounder.

A young Willie just found it interesting to hang out with the personalities at the caddie shack, first at Augusta Country Club, then at Augusta National. He enjoyed the card games and the competition of caddying against others. Stokes took him under his wing. Peterson was seventeen years old and a student at Haines Normal Industrial Institute when he started caddying in the Masters in 1949, for a different player every year.

By the early 1950s, Peterson was serving a stint in the U.S. Air Force. After a four-year term, it was back to Augusta and seemingly to a career in the funeral home business. An aunt, Annie Peterson, wanted Willie to succeed her in the family business. But Willie had other things in mind than dealing with dead bodies. While in the Air Force, he had developed a love of cooking, a talent he would take to a job in the kitchen at Augusta's University Hospital, later as a short-order cook at a restaurant in New York and during Masters Week in Augusta for various clients. Caddying was his main source of income, but it did not hurt to have alternatives.

Willie also had his eyes on fifteen-year-old Rosemary Allen, eight years his junior.

"He just starting coming around and he was one of the top eligible bachelors in the area," Rosemary says. "He was a

Caddie Willie Peterson *(left)* celebrates a birdie putt as Jack Nicklaus smiles during the 1965 Masters, Nicklaus' second Masters title. (© *Augusta Chronicle*)

very real, open person. Very free-hearted. Always smiling. A very, very, very aggressive person. Very positive. He could win you over like that."

The Petersons were married in 1955 and worked side by side in the kitchen at University Hospital. They went on to have six children over the next eleven years. Willie caddied and worked at the hospital.

Then, in 1959, Peterson struck secondhand gold.

Nicklaus was a hot-shot amateur that year in his Masters debut. The chubby nineteen-year-old junior at Ohio State University hit the ball a mile. He already had a reputation as an intense worker, both on the range and on the course. Caddies would have to spend their day shagging balls on the range, walking eighteen holes, working on the putting green and then back to the range to end the day. The caddies were not lined up to work for him. Pappy Stokes was the first to give Nicklaus a try.

"Jack Nicklaus was too slow for me," Pappy recalls. "I wanted somebody who would hit the ball and walk. I said, 'Pete, I'm going to give him to you.' Jack was paying good money, but he'd go out there at seven in the morning and come back at night. He'd stay out there all day on the practice field. I said, 'Man, you walked my legs off.' "

With input from his father, Charlie, Nicklaus was paired with Peterson.

Nicklaus was not looking for a caddie who could continuously club him or read his putts, just an assistant to be there in a time of need. Angelo Argea, Nicklaus' regular caddie on the PGA Tour for years, offered that characteristic, as did Dickinson, the Scotsman who loyally carried for Jack in the British Open during the 1960s and into the 1970s. They also offered luck—and lots of it.

Argea—full name Angelo George Argeropoulos—was a cab driver/caddie in Las Vegas in 1963 when he was picked by the tournament caddie master to work for Nicklaus, without Jack's approval, at the Bob Hope Desert Classic in Palm Springs, California. Angelo's long, wiry and wild crop of silver hair, thick mustache, dark complexion, and talkative nature drew comparisons to a Greek playboy, in stark contrast to the All-American image of Nicklaus' blond hair, fair complexion, and chunky build. But Jack won that Hope in a play-off with Gary Player, came to Vegas a few months later for the Tournament of Champions, and again in the fall for the Sahara Invitational. He captured the Desert Triple, each time with Angelo on the bag. So began a nearly twenty-year week-to-week relationship on Tour, except, of course, for the Masters, which Angelo never worked because of the ban on outside caddies.

But Jack had Willie at Augusta before he even met Angelo.

"All that I ask is a caddie be dependable," Nicklaus said in 1973. "As long as he's there on time to carry the bag, that's all I'm asking. That's absolutely the truth. Never has he hit any shots nor has he picked a club.

"I'm not saying a thing against Willie as a caddie. He gives me tremendous moral support ... I wouldn't trade him for a million dollars."

Peterson was the self-assured partner who could help with the little things. For instance, the twenty-three-year-old Nicklaus was on the way to the eighteenth green in the third round of his first Masters title in 1963. But Nicklaus could not figure out his standing with a quick glance at the big scoreboard to the right of the final green. Nicklaus is partly red-green color-blind and could not make out the scoring designations from more than 100 yards. He squinted to make out the green numerals that reflected over-par scores or the red ones that showed under-par scoring, two innovations that the Masters debuted to the golf world in the early 1960s. Nicklaus was 2-under par as he finished the round and a passel of players were at 1-over at the time, but Nicklaus did not know his leading margin.

"Willie, there's a lot of ones up there." Nicklaus asked, "How many of them are red?"

"Just you, boss," Peterson answered. "Those others are all green numbers."

In 1965, Nicklaus came to the seventeenth hole in the final round with a humongous lead. He was on the way to a record 17-under-par total and a nine-stroke victory margin. But the approach shot on the short par 4 had the tandem baffled. Nicklaus wanted to hit 9-iron and Peterson suggested a wedge.

"I'll hit it soft," Nicklaus said as Willie frowned.

Nicklaus proceeded to land his second shot within a foot for a tap-in birdie. Then he laughed, reached over, and pulled the bill of Willie's green baseball cap down over his caddie's eyes.

It was during this period when Jack was planning to chart the golf courses he played by yardage, a novel idea. By the 1963 Masters, Nicklaus would have a small notebook jammed in his back pocket for reference on various course landmarks that indicated distances to driving areas or greens. He was believed to be the first player to use such a system in a major championship. The course management Nicklaus became so famous for was already in process.

"This man don't miss a trick," Peterson said in 1970. "He walks off the course several times and puts down notes. When he pulls a club out, I don't question him. I know he is right."

In the early 1960s, Nicklaus was paired with Don January as they played the par-5 thirteenth hole. January had outdriven Nicklaus by 40 yards, leaving the thin Texan 190 yards to the green. Nicklaus, needing 230 yards to clear the creek that guards the green, debated with Peterson about strategy.

"I heard Willie tell Jack he didn't think he could get there (in two shots)," says Jariah Beard, the caddie for January that day and the bag man for Fuzzy Zoeller in his 1979 triumph. "Jack said, 'Gimme my 3-wood, I can hit it as far as I want to,' and he blistered it. It landed on the green. January turned around to me and said, 'He's going to run us all off the Tour,' which is basically what he did."

Peterson was not the great green reader like Carl Jackson or the expert course analyst like Pappy Stokes. Testimony to this comes in the fact that Bobby Mitchell used Peterson on his bag regularly on the PGA Tour in the early 1970s, and David Graham hired Peterson for the 1979 PGA Championship, both solely because they were steadfast in their desire to play the course without input, just like Jack. Both won with

Peterson on their bags. He was the ultimate motivator and comedic sidekick.

"Willie Peterson was just right for Jack Nicklaus," says Carl Jackson. "Nicklaus can do his own caddying. But Peterson was a good pep man. He was a good 'pat you on the back and let's go' man. He was good for Jack Nicklaus."

"Willie Peterson was a bag toter, but Jack Nicklaus liked him," Pappy says.

Hatcher says that "Peterson was just pure lucky" to get Nicklaus. Nevertheless, that luck transformed into a twenty-four-year relationship that carried Peterson all over the world.

"I remember when I first got Mr. Jack, I knew I had a winner," Peterson said in the early 1970s. "I figured he'd win ten Masters before he was through. I considered myself lucky—I had sort of an annuity."

Peterson gave Nicklaus the touch of humor that occasionally broke the intense four hours of work during a Masters round. He once told Nicklaus, "Mr. Jack, I need to have more than anyone's ever been paid."

When Nicklaus arrived at the practice range at midday Sunday before the final round of the 1975 Masters, Peterson was waiting there with Jack's big green MacGregor golf bag. But he was not his usual chatty self. He just stared at Nicklaus' feet.

"I still had my street shoes on," Nicklaus said. "Willie just cracked, 'Did you forget something boss?' "

He also served as a buffer for some of the negative feedback from Arnie's Army, which resented the fact that this fat kid from Ohio had stolen the spotlight from their hero. They labeled the rotund Nicklaus of the 1960s with unfavorable nicknames such as "Blobbo," "Ohio Fats," "Baby Beef," and the more familiar "Fat Jack." Willie's position when a gallery member or two would voice some displeasure was to "just smile and keep on fighting."

Unlike his caddie comrades, Willie also kept up with Jack. He arrived on time and stayed until the day was done. He would backpedal until he hit the bushes at the far end of the Augusta National practice range while shagging balls and watch as Nicklaus rocketed drives over his head into Washington Road, with the gallery oohing and ahhing and other Masters participants stopping their warm-up sessions to watch the display. Willie would play up the scene some 275 yards into the distance by whirling his towel over his head, like an umpire signaling to circle the bases because it is a home run.

Like Iron Man just a few years before him, Peterson became a celebrity in Augusta's black community. That spilled over to the white areas, too, particularly the restaurants and bars that were building up along Washington Road in the late 1960s and 1970s. Most establishments prominently displayed Masters memorabilia, and Jack was always there, more times than not with Willie right by his side in the photographs.

But his Big Man About Town persona did not always translate into a happy home life.

In April 1966, Nicklaus was the defending champion in the Masters. As was his normal practice, Willie would take a bag lunch from Rosemary and then pick up his brother Godfrey, who also caddied at Augusta National, on the way to the course.

It was the Monday of Masters Week and the children were out of school for spring break. By the time Willie's car disappeared down the street bound for Augusta National, Rosemary was packing up the family, and they bolted out of town for New York. She was tired of Willie's extreme jealousy and his penchant for staying out too late, usually gambling or hustling, and wasting the money he had earned while caddying for Nicklaus over the early part of the 1960s. He provided clothes and food for the children and got them away from the "ghetto fabulous" people in Dogwood Terrace, a housing development in South Augusta. However, she thought they could do much better. Rosemary figured that with Willie working for Nicklaus in the Masters that week, it would be the opportune time to leave. Willie would not follow them.

"I got married so young, and he was good to me," Rosemary says. "I just felt like we were missing out on a lot of things. I wanted something different. So, I decided we should move on. He eventually accepted that. And we both moved on."

Vanessa Peterson-Fox *(left)* and her brother Russell Peterson are two of Willie Peterson's children. Willie lived with Vanessa in Augusta for a short period during the later years of his life. Russell at one time was organizing some type of fundraiser for the old Augusta National caddies. Willie died in 1999. (Photograph by Rob Carr, © *Augusta Chronicle*)

In tow were the six children, who would see their father off and on over the next two decades. Rosemary remarried, to Arthur Marshall Sr., a military man, and eventually came back to Augusta. Willie moved to Savannah for a period, where he started a relationship with another woman. At one point, the children did not see their father for five or six years when they moved to Germany in the 1970s. They once stumbled upon a *Newsweek* magazine on the newsstands in Europe that had a story on the Masters. Prominently pictured was Nicklaus with Willie right by his side.

Along the way, tragedy struck two of the older children. Tyrone, the oldest boy, was stationed in the army at Fort Bragg, North Carolina. While playing in a basketball game on base in 1974, he passed out and died from a heart defect. Pondra, the oldest daughter, died at age forty in 1997 of an aneurysm.

Most prominently, daughter Vanessa's relationship with her father speaks volumes about the feelings in the young black community of the 1970s toward the Masters. By the time she had returned to Augusta at age sixteen in the mid-1970s, Vanessa had seen the world through her stepfather's frequent moves as a military man. A few years later, she was prepared to go off to college at Georgia Southern University in nearby Statesboro, Georgia. The black power movement and race riots of the 1960s in the South had hit home hard for her generation.

"Being an educated woman and having traveled the world, I have a very, very strong sense of worth," Vanessa, forty-four, says. "It took me some time to understand that my parents came from a different time. I just didn't think being a caddie was such a thing I'd want to brag about. My dad participated and worked for a club where initially blacks couldn't even play golf there. I think now about all the attention Augusta National is getting about not having a woman member. It took such a long time for a black man to play there and become a member there. Daddy worked there since the 1950s. I got a sense he was in a situation where, 'You can work for us but you can't work beside us.'

"Daddy was all hot and heavy about how great golf and caddying was. I didn't think caddies were really that important, that they didn't contribute much. I thought, 'How can you be proud of carrying a real big bag of golf clubs around for a guy?' I didn't realize they really make a contribution to the player. I just said I'm moving on to better things."

Willie encouraged his daughter to learn how to play the game. He even tried to introduce her to Nicklaus and get her a job with his vastly expanding company. But she went her own way. She married young also, in college, and began a life of her own as Vanessa Peterson-Fox.

Caddie Willie Peterson sits on the front porch of the Augusta National Golf Club after Jack Nicklaus was forced to withdraw from the 1983 Masters because of back spasms. It would be Peterson's last Masters with Nicklaus. (© *Augusta Chronicle*)

About this same time, Willie's relationship on the course with Nicklaus was near its end. Willie closed in on age fifty in the early 1980s, had put on a lot of weight, and smoked too many cigarettes. While Jack had transformed from Blobbo to a sleek, stylish golfer in the 1970s, Willie morphed from a sturdy, athletic man into a heavy-set, near-sighted, middle-aged caddie. When outside caddies were allowed to work the 1983 Masters, most players opted to bring their own people. Nicklaus did not, keeping Willie on his bag. Nicklaus even opted to have Willie work the 1982 PGA Championship at Southern Hills in Tulsa, Oklahoma, where Nicklaus finished in a tie for sixteenth. Unfortunately, the 1983 Masters was cut short when Nicklaus suffered a back injury and had to withdraw before the second round. He tried to tee it up, but could not make a full swing.

When Nicklaus officially withdrew from that Masters, Willie was sitting on the front porch of Augusta National's clubhouse, virtually hugging Jack's golf bag. He was near tears.

"Playing bad doesn't make me sad," Willie said. "I'm more sad when anything happens to him. Anything happens to him, happens to me. I've been around him for twenty-five years. I feel like part of me left, too. Fact, it is."

It was the last Masters for the team of Jack and Willie. Michael Downey was on Nicklaus' bag in 1984. Nicklaus tried to keep Willie in the fold by bringing him to Florida to work in various Nicklaus golf holdings, first as the caddie master at the new Loxahatchee Golf Club in Jupiter, Florida, in 1985 and 1986. But Willie was his old self, getting into trouble with what one person said was "taking bribes." Things did not work out well at a couple other stops within the Nicklaus empire. Willie even tried to caddie there some, but suffered a severely pinched nerve in his back in the process, an injury that forced him to sleep on the floor or sitting up for much of the rest of his life.

Willie came back to Augusta briefly after the failure in Florida. His last real connection with Nicklaus occurred in 1986. He was watching the final round of the Masters on television with Vanessa, since divorced and living in Augusta, when

Nicklaus began to charge. Willie went to Augusta National and watched some of the back nine.

"If he shoots 30 (on the back nine), they can hang it up," Peterson said to no one in particular as he watched Jack play Amen Corner that Sunday. Sure enough, Jack shot that number and won by one stroke, at age forty-six. Willie Peterson, age fifty-three, had seemingly touched the sixth Masters title after guiding the first five.

From there, the rest of Willie Peterson's life is somewhat of a mystery. Augusta was not big enough to hold him. He got into financial trouble there and opted in the early 1990s to move to New York, where numerous relatives resided. He moved into a building with a majority of senior citizens. In search of work, he basically became a runner for a loan shark, a genteel-looking older white man. In a tight situation, this man probably could have put some serious pressure on his "clients," Willie included, but he liked Willie, just as everybody else did. Willie ran the numbers, delivered money, whatever was necessary to make a living. The fast pace of New York made his heart beat faster, but also probably got the best of him.

"My dad was a hustler," Vanessa says. "When I say a hustler, I mean he did whatever it took to make money, to survive. On the flip side, he was as sweet-hearted as he could be. He always said that if you had money in your hand and just hold it tight, nothing can go out, but guess what, nothing can come in either. He just lived. During the course of his life, he never worried about savings. If my father had $1,000 and you were sitting in here and needed some of that badly, he would give it to you. I didn't understand, but that's the way he was. He was on ol' kook."

Willie's health deteriorated quickly. He was diagnosed with throat cancer, which prohibited him from speaking clearly. Vanessa, in Augusta, had difficulty communicating with him via long-distance phone calls, eventually learning his groans and squeaks as a form of language. By 1998, the cancer had spread to his lungs. Vanessa did not realize the severity of the situation.

"I knew he was sick, but not that sick," Vanessa said. "It was a shock when (Willie) died."

Willie died on March 20, 1999, at age sixty-six, broke, in a rundown New York apartment. He had discovered something that would defeat him, cancer. Vanessa got word from New York by phone.

What followed over the next few months was, in many ways, a catharsis for Vanessa. The girl who had scorned her father's profession realized what kind of pleasure and notoriety he had developed by simply toting a golf bag. She was the child with the closest relationship to her father and took the responsibility to give him a fitting burial.

Her first chore was to find her father's body. Over the phone, she called various New York City hospitals. Finally, she found him, two days after his death. At first, she thought about going to New York, but then realized it was best to fly his body home. She asked her cousins to not touch anything in Willie's apartment, in case there were old belongings or Masters memorabilia, but anything of value was gone.

The only problem was that Vanessa could not afford to pay the nearly $1,000 tab to get his father's body flown back to Augusta. Combine that with a myriad of other problems. Her son, born with a congenital heart defect, had recently undergone a fourth heart operation at age nine. Her job at a local department store, J.B. White, was an on-again, off-again proposition because of a recent buyout by Dillard's. Her stepfather had passed away from cancer eight months prior and older sister Pondra and a grandmother died eighteen months before. To complicate matters, Willie's life insurance policy had not been paid up.

What to do? Close friends suggested that she call Nicklaus, a man she had only met once years ago and just briefly. Unknown to Vanessa, when her older brother Tyrone died suddenly in 1974, Nicklaus sent a check for $1,000 to Willie. When Willie became very ill in the late 1990s, Nicklaus sent a wheelchair to assist his former caddie. Those were just two of the known generous offerings.

"I was desperate, so I got on the phone and called this

number," Vanessa recalls. "I talked to Mr. Nicklaus' secretary, explained who I was and what had happened. They overnighted me a check for $1,000. That just blew me away. This man didn't even know me and Daddy worked for him years ago, yet he cared enough to send this money. We got him home."

With the recent burden of multiple deaths in the family, Vanessa wanted to celebrate her father's life instead of mourning again. "I was tired of death and dying, I wanted to remember my father with a smile on my face," Vanessa says. At the wake, held on March 27, 1999, at C.A. Reid Memorial Funeral Home, many of the old Augusta National caddies came to reminisce about Willie and their caddying days. Nicklaus sent a huge flower arrangement. They played a highlight tape, provided by The Golf Channel, of the 1975 Masters. Photos of Willie as a caddie were on display.

"I always had reservations about what Dad did because I didn't live here," Vanessa says. "But these people came to that wake, people who had worked with him, and went on and on about him. I haven't run into one person who didn't like him. He had a great personality."

The affect of those last rites made a big impact on Vanessa and Russell, the youngest Peterson.

Just two years old when Rosemary bolted town with the children in 1966, Russell's only impression of his father's trade was once seeing a huge bag of money after a Nicklaus victory in the Masters. "That must be some kind of job," he thought. He takes after Willie in that he likes to cook and bears a strong physical resemblance to his late father. Today, Russell is a booking agent who works to bring singing acts to the Augusta area. He was previously a real estate agent in Augusta and was trying to organize a fund-raising golf tournament for the old caddies at Augusta National. He met with a group of them a few times and wanted to unveil the program only when it was ready to be a big deal, not just a piecemeal arrangement.

"Those guys deserve something like this," Russell says. "They gave their lives to caddie at Augusta National."

Nearly one year after her father's death, Vanessa was driving down Washington Road and saw some Masters memorabilia for sale at a roadside stand. For some reason, she stopped to look. There was a huge painting of the 1975 Masters, with (as usual) Willie Peterson smack dab in the middle of the action. The cost: $1,500.

"I felt like crying right then," she says. "I couldn't afford that. I never knew his worth and never gave him credit for what he did. On some level, Daddy used to brag, just like my ex-husband used to brag, about catching a big fish. I used to just say, 'Yeah right.' It just dawned on me when I saw that picture that my dad was really a part of something great."

Yes, Willie Peterson was a character. And he had character, too.

Willie Beats Jack

About the only person who could beat Jack Nicklaus in 1972 was somebody with Willie Peterson on the bag.

Jack was age thirty-two, considerably slimmed down from his previous "Fat Jack" look, and in his prime, winning seven times in twenty starts (including four runner-up finishes) in 1972 and nearly capturing the Grand Slam after winning the Masters and U.S. Open and then finishing second to Lee Trevino at the British Open. It was Nicklaus' second of four consecutive years as the leading money winner on the PGA Tour and the second of five years that he earned PGA of America Player of the Year honors. Nicklaus ruled golf.

So it was no surprise that Jack won the '72 Masters. He coasted to the wire-to-wire victory, finishing at 2-under-par 286, the only man under par on an Augusta National course that had extremely bumpy and unpredictable Bermuda grass greens that year because of infestation by Poa annua. It was Nicklaus' fourth Masters title, tying Arnold Palmer for the most in tournament history, and all came with Peterson by his side.

One player three back in a three-way tie for second was Bobby Mitchell, a journeyman pro from Danville, Virginia, who would be a blip on Nicklaus' radar screen a couple weeks later. Mitchell, playing in just his second Masters, may have finished a bit closer to Jack except that he played the testy par-3 twelfth hole in 5-over par during the tournament.

The twenty-nine-year-old Mitchell was quite an interesting story. He quit school in the tenth grade at age fifteen in 1958 because "I wasn't getting good grades and anyway I spent more time on the golf course than in the classroom." He immediately became an assistant pro at Danville Country Club, began playing in PGA Sectional events at age twenty-two, and then tried his wares on the PGA Tour in the late 1960s. He won the 1971 Cleveland Open Invitational, shooting 26-under-par 262 to win by seven strokes. Therefore, Mitchell had game, even if he called himself golf's "Invisible Man."

"(CBS broadcaster) Ken Venturi says I'm the most underrated player on the Tour," Mitchell said in 1972. "Maybe I'm too plain. I don't throw my clubs. I don't wear colorful clothes."

As a gag late in 1971, he purchased a toupee to cover his balding head when he was not wearing his golf hat.

"I got to liking it and it felt good, so I just leave it on all the time now," Mitchell said then. "I think it looks good."

Most importantly, he had Nicklaus' caddie. Willie Peterson worked solely for Jack in the Masters, but was employed by an assortment of pros during the rest of the Tour schedule over the years. Jack's regular caddie, Angelo Argea, worked virtually everywhere else outside caddies were allowed.

"I can't remember exactly when and where, but Willie just walked up to me on Tour one day late in 1971 and we started working together," says Mitchell today at age sixty and still playing occasionally on the Champions Tour. "I didn't have a regular caddie when I won at Cleveland. Then Willie and I worked together for the next two years.

"Willie was a good caddie, a real character. Let me just say he wasn't a quiet person. He was talking all the time. That was his way of doing things.

"I was the type of player who did his own work, I guess sort of like Jack did. All (Peterson) had to do was back up the yardage. I read my own putts. Basically, what he did was carry the bag and keep me loose. He didn't have a hard job."

The irony was that two weeks after finishing second to Nicklaus at the 1972 Masters, Mitchell had Peterson on his bag in the Tournament of Champions at La Costa Resort and Spa in Carlsbad, California. The tournament, for winners of Tour events for the previous calendar year, drew the elite of the sport to the ritzy Southern California resort.

As the final round came on April 23, Mitchell trailed Nicklaus by two strokes. Mitchell fired a 2-under-par 70 in the final round to catch Nicklaus at 8-under-par 280, forcing a sudden-death play-off.

"I didn't think anything about Willie working for Jack all that time," Mitchell says. "I had enough other stuff to think about playing against Jack."

On the first play-off hole, the par-3 seventeenth, Nicklaus pulled his tee shot into the left rough and his second shot would not hold the quick green. Mitchell ended the match quickly, sinking a twenty-foot birdie putt for the biggest win of his career and the biggest upset on Tour in years.

"Don't ever do that again," Barbara Nicklaus, Jack's wife, jokingly told Peterson after Mitchell's win. "If you need some money, come to me."

By 1973, Mitchell had lost his Tour exemption and the association with Peterson was no more.

"When you had a regular caddie then, you had to pay them a regular salary," Mitchell says. "When I wasn't playing regularly, that was too expensive. So he had to go find another regular job."

David and Willie at the PGA

Willie Peterson's penchant for being an outwardly proud man was never more evident than in the 1979 PGA Championship at Oakland Hills Country Club in Birmingham, Michigan.

Peterson becoming the only Augusta National–bred caddie to win in a major tournament other than the Masters is only a small part of the story that took place late that summer.

Australian David Graham chose the forty-seven-year-old

Peterson, a five-time Masters Tournament winner on Nicklaus' bag, to caddie for him that week because, in large part, he wanted to closely emulate the self-guidance of Nicklaus. Jack had become famous for calculating yardages, reading putts, and choosing clubs without relying on input from a caddie.

"It became a status thing to play like Jack did," Graham recalled in a March 2001 *Golf Digest* interview.

Graham, at age thirty-three, was in the final round of his life at Oakland Hills, billed as "The Monster" by Ben Hogan during his 1951 U.S. Open victory there. Graham was near the end of a furious rally to come from four strokes behind third-round leader Rex Caldwell as he stood on the tee of the 459-yard, dogleg right par-4 eighteenth hole with a two-stroke lead over Ben Crenshaw. Graham was 7-under par for the day, cruising to a major championship record-tying round of 63. To boot, a magazine offer of $50,000 for breaking the course record and another $50,000 for breaking the tournament record hung in the balance if Graham could just make a final par. The additional $100,000 would exceed the $60,000 winner's prize for the PGA champion.

With visions of the Wannamaker Trophy dancing in his head, Graham's drive sailed wildly to the right. Being like Jack had worked like a charm all week, so as Graham found his errant tee shot he began to figure what he had remaining from the unusual position in the right rough. Playing partners Jerry Pate and Caldwell were patient as Graham attempted to get his bearings. The converted par 5 usually required a driver and long iron to reach the green. However, this was a completely different angle. As he walked toward the fairway, Graham could not clear the large gallery enough to locate a sprinkler head that would indicate the distance for his second shot.

He walked back to his ball. Finally, he asked for Peterson's input.

"How far is it?" Graham blurted out as he studied the second shot.

Peterson quickly spouted off: "You haven't asked me one

question all the way around. I don't know. Figure it out yourself."

"Excuse me?" was all that Graham could muster in response as he stared incredulously at his caddie.

Obviously shaken, he eventually pulled a 6-iron and blew the second shot over the green, then badly dubbed a chip from the thick rough onto the fringe, chipped on in four, and missed a four-foot bogey putt to record a double-bogey. Forget the record final round and bonus money, Graham settled for a 65 and was headed for a sudden-death play-off with Crenshaw, tied at 8-under-par 272.

Peterson charged up as they left the final green.

"Don't worry, Boss, we'll get 'em in the play-off," a suddenly supportive Peterson offered.

"Don't even speak to me," a furious Graham said as he prepared to enter the scorer's tent. "The farther you stay away from me, the happier I'll be. Just carry the clubs."

Graham apparently was headed toward the biggest choke job in PGA Championship history. The gallery around the first tee was soundly in Ben's corner. Crenshaw split the first fairway in the play-off and Graham duck-hooked his drive. Graham was blocked from going for the green, had to lay up, then hit a poor chip to within twenty-five feet. Crenshaw made a standard two-putt par. But Graham miraculously holed the twenty-five-footer for par to extend the play-off.

On the par-5 second hole, Graham canned a ten-footer for birdie to stay alive as Crenshaw two-putted for birdie. Then, on the third extra hole, a par 3, after Crenshaw's approach found a bunker, Graham holed a four-foot birdie putt to win his first major title. A huge sigh of relief came to both player and caddie, although separately.

"If you watch the tape—you know how the caddies usually run and hug the player and do all of that kind of stuff?—you'll see a lot of apprehension before I put my arms around Willie," Graham said.

The First Timer

It is your first Masters Tournament and you can get just one practice round in at Augusta National. Only one month prior, at San Diego, you won for the first time on the PGA Tour to earn a trip to Augusta.

What lies ahead for twenty-seven-year-old Frank Urban Zoeller, better known as Fuzzy? Should he go ahead and reserve a Friday night flight out of town from the 1979 Masters? Or just cherish how beautiful the flowers are for a couple days?

No, Zoeller opts to put all of his rookie trust in a caddie, Jariah Beard, a longtime caddie at Augusta National. He did not have another choice.

"This is your course, tell me what to hit and I'll hit it," Zoeller told Beard.

Beard had caddied for veteran Don January since 1967. But Mike Shannon, one of Augusta National's assistant professionals at the time, was a regular in Beard's foursome every Monday at Forest Hills Golf Club. Shannon also was a roommate of Zoeller's at the University of Houston. He set them up before the tournament, in hopes that Beard could give his friend some pointers.

When Beard reported to work on the Monday before Masters Week, caddie master Freddie Bennett told Beard, "You don't have January anymore. Your buddy Shannon got you a bag."

Bennett would not reveal the name until later in the day. It did not matter.

"What in the heck is a Fuzzy Zoeller? I don't know anything about him," Beard said.

Fuzzy, who earned his nickname from his initials (F.U.Z.), was a laid-back pro from New Albany, Indiana, who loved to joke with the gallery and whistle while he worked on the golf course. He had played most of his career with a painful back injury suffered as a high school sophomore in the mid-1960s

Caddie Jariah Beard *(center)* and Fuzzy Zoeller *(right)* rejoice after Zoeller's birdie on the eleventh hole in a sudden-death play-off gave him the 1979 Masters title. Zoeller joined Harmon Smith, the tournament's first winner, and Gene Sarazen, the 1935 champion, as the only first-time participants to win the event. In this photo Beard is looking heavenward because Zoeller tossed his putter in the air when he made the winning birdie putt. Ed Sneed *(left)* is seen in the background. (© *Augusta Chronicle*)

on the basketball team in hoops-crazy Indiana. When he drove to the basket in a game, Zoeller jumped, had his legs cut out from under him, and came down smack dab on the back of his neck, suffering damage that would later require surgery. Since joining the PGA Tour in 1974, Zoeller had increasingly inched up the money list, topped by his five-stroke victory in the Andy Williams–San Diego Open Invitational early in 1979.

He came to Augusta without his wife, Diane, who was at home expecting their first child, daughter Sunnye, within the next three weeks.

"I just like to play golf, and I think finishing fourth is better than fifth, and finishing fifteenth is better than sixteenth," Zoeller said early in the week.

Things worked out perfectly. Zoeller was never in the news and only within shouting distance of pacesetter Ed Sneed until the very end. The reason he was still in contention was Beard's input.

"He led me around like I was a blind man," Zoeller said years later. "That seeing-eye dog was great. He told me where to hit it and where not to hit it. He told me on the par 5s when to go for it in two shots and when to lay up. Those guys know.

"I was fortunate I was playing well at the time and I was able to hit it where he told me to. I'm still trying to hit those damn areas, but the ball doesn't want to cooperate. It's the ball's fault, I'm convinced of that."

Zoeller started the final round at 6-under par, in a tie for fourth, six strokes behind Sneed. He was paired with Tom Watson in the next-to-last group of the day. "I was just trying to stay close to Watson, who's not a bad guy to stay close to," Zoeller said.

Fuzzy cruised around the course, seemingly nonchalant about the revered back nine at Augusta National on a Sunday. The biggest shot may have come on the 500-yard, par-5 fifteenth. Faced with a 235-yard 3-wood second shot into the wind, Zoeller wanted to lay up in front of the pond that guards the front of the green. Beard objected.

First off, know that Beard was not afraid of giving his opinion. In his Masters caddying debut as a sixteen-year-old in 1957, Beard worked for Bob Toski. On the twelfth hole in the second round, Toski asked Beard for his club selection on the tricky par 3 and he offered a 6-iron. As playing partner Doug Sanders, with the honor on the tee, chose a 7-iron, Beard wavered. Toski pulled a 7-iron, hit his tee shot short into Rae's Creek, and missed the cut, first instituted that year, by one stroke.

"Don't ever let anyone influence you on what to do," Beard remembers Toski lecturing him after the round. "(Toski) just said to make up your mind and stick to your own opinion. That's the way I've always been as a caddie ever since. Do what you want, but this is what I think."

The influence of the week with Zoeller had come down to this moment on No. 15.

"If you're gonna have any chance to win, you've got to go for it," Beard said.

"But there's no way I can hit the 3-wood that far into the wind," Fuzzy came back.

From the nearby gallery came another voice of authority. Fuzzy's father was listening in on the conversation.

"Son, he hasn't been wrong all week," Mr. Zoeller said. "Go ahead and do what he tells you."

Zoeller drilled the 3-wood and blindly asked Beard to tell him the result, half expecting a watery answer. Instead, the ball found the green and Zoeller two-putted for birdie. "How far can I hit a 3-wood? 235 yards without any wind. I don't know how it got there," Zoeller said. He needed to gamble because he was four behind Sneed. Another Zoeller birdie on the par-4 seventeenth put him 2-under over the last four holes and seemingly in position for a great finish.

Zoeller waited behind the eighteenth green after signing his scorecard for an 8-under-par 280 total, tied with Watson for the clubhouse lead. Zoeller and Beard watched as Sneed three-putted the par-3 sixteenth and failed to get up and down from behind the green on the par-4 seventeenth. Then they saw Sneed miss the green short on the par-4 eighteenth and chip to within six feet.

"Get ready to go to ten. He doesn't know this putt," Beard told Zoeller quietly as Sneed lined up his par putt.

Sneed's miss forced the first sudden-death play-off in Masters history, going down the tenth hole. All three players made simple two-putt pars there, sending the match to the par-4 eleventh. Normally, the caddies hand the players their drivers and then take a shortcut down the right side of the fairway to await the drives. But Zoeller asked Beard to accompany him to the tee box, set back and to the left of the tenth green.

"Give me a new nugget, Jariah," Zoeller said. "I want to beat high ball-hitting Tom Watson here. I don't want to play him on twelve."

Zoeller cranked his longest drive of the week, leaving two less clubs into the green than Watson or Sneed. Sneed's 5-iron found the back bunker, Watson played a 6-iron to within eighteen feet, and Zoeller zeroed in on the flag, hitting a knock-down 8-iron to within six feet. Sneed nearly holed his bunker shot and Watson missed his birdie putt. That set up Zoeller's short birdie putt.

"Two balls right and don't leave it short," was Beard's last direction for Zoeller's winning putt.

When Fuzzy's ball disappeared into the hole, he tossed his Ping Zing putter in the air, forgetting to retrieve it afterwards. Beard, sitting on Zoeller's bag to the left of the eleventh green, immediately jumped up and raised his eyes to the heavens, possibly giving thanks for some kind of divine intervention but more likely to keep Zoeller's putter from cracking somebody on the head. He nearly caught the putter before it landed on the green. They had teamed to make Zoeller the first rookie winner since Gene Sarazen in 1935. Technically, inaugural tournament winner Horton Smith was also a rookie victor.

Zoeller forked over more than ten percent of his $50,000 first-place check to Beard that day. He also handed over the bright orange Powerbilt golf bag, which Beard has stored away in his attic. They continued to work together through 1982, but when outside caddies were allowed to work at the Masters in 1983, it was the end of the Beard-Zoeller team.

Originally, Zoeller was going to retain Beard over his regular Tour caddie, Mike Mazzeo. However, on the Friday before the 1983 tournament, Zoeller changed course.

"He told me, 'I've got to play with those guys on the Tour every week, live with them and travel with them,' " Beard said. "In other words, he was going to get some flak from other pros if he didn't go with them (on using Tour caddies)."

"I'm lucky that I had a very good caddie at Augusta," Zoeller said. "We always got along well, but you see them (Augusta National caddies) only one time a year and it's hard to build up confidence that way."

With the end of their association, it was also the finale of Beard's caddying days. He began concentrating on his full-time job with Continental Can (now International Paper), an occupation he had started in 1966 to support his wife and five children. Previously, Beard would voluntarily switch to the night shift when alerted by Bennett that one of his regular member bags would be available the next day, making for a long night of work, an early morning breakfast, and then sometimes thirty-six holes as a caddie. Caddying at Augusta National was a passion, but not an end all. The 1982 Masters was his last as an Augusta National employee.

"When I can't make the money that really counts, hey, I'll go do something else," Beard said.

He was urged by Bennett to come back to work part-time at Augusta National a few years ago, but Beard declined because the new caddie selection system may have relegated him to waiting around all day and not receiving a bag. The only caddying he does today is the occasional visit to Sage Valley Golf Club, a new ultra-exclusive golf club across the Savannah River in South Carolina, to work for Larry McCrary, a former Augusta National member. He is also known to tutor his playing partners during frequent casual rounds at the Augusta Golf Course, the city's municipal course better known as "The Cabbage Patch" for its former rag-tag conditioning.

Beard, now sixty-two, serves as the unofficial historian for Augusta National caddies. He can recall given names for caddie nicknames and family members or recite the influence caddies had on winning players' games. After all, he took the usual route to the caddie yards at Augusta National: raised in the Sand Hill section of Augusta, apprentice caddie at Augusta Country Club at age eleven, "graduation" to Augusta National a few years later, and then a steady job in the Masters for nearly twenty-five years for a variety of players.

"We were such a part of it, a tradition at that time," Beard said. "It was about how well you caddied. It showed in the tournament. If you pulled a bad club or read a bad green, you heard about it from the rest of the caddies. We took pride in what we did. It wasn't like just another job. It was something we really, really loved doing."

Zoeller did have a bit of a situation with Mazzeo a couple years after bringing him to Augusta. On Thursday night after the first round, a call came from one of the local hospitals at 10 P.M. Mazzeo had a "hot date" after one of Augusta's many Masters Week parties and was headed back to his hotel room. However, his key would not open the door, so he tried to kick through the plate-glass window and severely cut his Achilles tendon, thereby benching him for the week. In stepped Fuzzy's older brother.

"Eddie Joe was a very weak caddie," Zoeller said with a laugh. "I drove it in the bunker on No. 1 and going down the fairway, he said, 'I ain't raking no traps, brother.' Then I hit it in the trees on No. 2 and he said, 'I'm not going in the woods. And I'm not putting any pelts (divots) back either.' Yep, he was a weak caddie. But he was cheap. I just had to pay him six cold beers a round. And we yukked it up the whole time."

Even though Beard and Zoeller see each other only every couple of years and had an uneasy breakup, they still have the bond of 1979. When Zoeller uttered his infamous "fried chicken and collard greens" statement in 1997 about Tiger Woods' probable Champions Dinner menu the following year, Beard had a different take than most critics on the controversy.

"The whole thing was I think Fuzzy had been drinking," Beard said of the sound bite caught on CNN. "In the spotlight, you've got to be careful what you say. I feel like if Fuzzy had walked up to Tiger and said that face-to-face privately, they both would have laughed about it, as a joke, and walked on. But that should have been a private conversation, not in the public limelight."

Zoeller still contends that first-timers in the Masters should use Augusta National caddies. He is the poster boy for that advice.

"Personally, I think all first-time guys should use a caddie around here all the time just because they know the greens," Zoeller said. "I understand players have their caddies around all year long and feel like they owe it to them. But if I am caddying for a first-time player at the Masters, I step aside and become a spectator."

Ben and Carl: The Bond

This picture reveals their character. The years spent on the road, away from family, struggling to make a living, then making it. A soft-spoken gentleman overcoming a death sentence. That is Carl Jackson, in the caddie outfit, on the left. The promise of being the next Nicklaus, the man with a see-saw golf game, respected as a historian, leader, all-around nice guy and Hall of Famer. That is Ben Crenshaw, filled with emotion, on the right.

It is April 9, 1995, a warm spring Sunday afternoon as dusk approaches in the final round of the Masters Tournament. Seven days have transformed personal hell into a triumph far beyond simply winning a golf tournament. More prominently, it is the embodiment of good men who worked hard to make things happen, and it comes raining down on them.

Crenshaw, age forty-three, came to Augusta the weekend prior with a golf game in shambles. A slightly built man at five-feet-nine, 157 pounds, he needs all parts of his golf swing in sync to manufacture the power and consistency necessary to keep up with the younger, longer hitters of the day. The long, flowing putting stroke, with his cherished putter, "Gentle Ben," has carried his game through the years, but cannot shoulder this big a burden. Ben has missed the cut in three of the previous four tournaments, including a short title defense the week before in New Orleans at the Freeport-McMoRan Classic. His right big toe is throbbing from a calcium deposit suffered years earlier when he hauled off and kicked a trashcan out of anger following a poor round at some faraway tournament. Crenshaw's ball striking fit a bad double bill: short and crooked.

Just as Crenshaw feels this on-course despair, his longtime instructor, Harvey Penick, passes away in Austin, Texas, their hometown, at age ninety, the Sunday before the Masters begins. Crenshaw has just completed a casual practice round at quiet, peaceful Augusta National, with wife Julie strolling alongside, when he gets word of Penick's death. Tom Kite calls from Austin to interrupt the Crenshaws' dinner in the Augusta National clubhouse. It is not an unexpected call, but still a shock to the system.

What Crenshaw, his Texas sidekick Kite, and numerous other noted golf professionals had for years listened to in awe recently had become public domain. In Harvey's latter years, his down-home instructional tips were published and critically acclaimed, most notably in Harvey Penick's *Little Red Book,* an all-time best seller.

When Penick was teaching a young Crenshaw the game, he noticed the budding natural talent and sent Ben forth with an unusual rule. Ben was not to practice too much "for fear that he might find out how to do something wrong."

Penick was so basic in his teaching method. There was no technical mumbo-jumbo to create paralysis by analysis in his pupils. Instead, Harvey's teachings provided guidance through the game's toughest moments. He would state adages such as:

"A good putter is a match for anyone. A bad putter is a match for no one. The woods are full of long drivers."

"Arnold Palmer likes to grip the club tightly, but you are not Arnold Palmer."

On the last Sunday in March 1995, Harvey was virtually on his deathbed at home. Crenshaw was over for possibly a last visit before taking off to play at New Orleans that week.

Ben Crenshaw is consoled by caddie Carl Jackson after Crenshaw holed out on the eighteenth hole to complete his victory in the 1995 Masters. Crenshaw overcame the death of his longtime mentor Harvey Penick the week before the tournament and was assisted by a couple of simple tips from Jackson on the driving range during tournament week. (© *Augusta Chronicle*)

The talk turned to golf and the state of Ben's game. Harvey commanded that Crenshaw go to the garage and fetch Harvey's trusty old wooden Gene Sarazen putter. He wanted to check Ben's grip, the same grip Harvey had formed when Ben was just age six. After a brief glimpse, Harvey simply instructed, "Just trust yourself." Ten days later, Harvey's son, Tinsley, the head professional at Austin Country Club, would present Ben the putter after his father's funeral.

The thought of Harvey's loss piles onto Crenshaw's already fragile emotions as he tries to focus on the Masters Tournament at hand. Always an emotional sort, this could create the boiling point.

Funeral plans were set for Wednesday, the day before the first round of the Masters. Any intense practice time to recover a semblance of a golf game would have to be compacted into two days' work.

So Crenshaw stood on the practice tee uncharacteristically beating balls on Tuesday afternoon, trying to find a simple swing key. Only hours later, a private jet would depart Augusta bound for Austin so that he and Kite could serve as pallbearers at Penick's funeral. Frustration is setting in. Crenshaw slowly shakes his head and his shoulders drop as he glances toward any close-by observers.

"I just see two things," Jackson, age forty-eight, volunteers suddenly from about fifteen feet behind the golfer, perched atop Crenshaw's horizontal King Cobra golf bag. "Try something ... Put the ball back in your stance and make a tighter turn with your shoulders."

Crenshaw listens. He is used to Jackson reminding him about timing and tempo, course strategy, or the wide arc for the line of a putt, but nothing quite this technical, especially put forth so forcefully. The ball position slips back a hair in Crenshaw's stance. He concentrates on a backswing where his arms are not separated from his body as much.

Whack ... whack ... whack. Magic.

"A light went off," Crenshaw says. "Two or three swings and I was making contact like I hadn't felt in a long time."

Was it Carl, or mystically, Harvey speaking?

"I guess you could say it was just like something Harvey would have told me, short, simple, and direct," Crenshaw says. "Carl knows me like Harvey knew me."

So Crenshaw headed to Austin for the funeral. Even though filled with sadness that Wednesday morning, he displayed a certain glow.

"How you doin'?" older brother Charlie inquires after Penick's burial. "You've got a different kind of look on your face."

"*We* found something," Crenshaw says. "I can't wait to get back to Augusta and try it."

In Ben's head from the first tee Thursday onward is Penick's mantra, "Take dead aim." In his ear is Jackson, the longtime sidekick whose soothing, quiet voice belies his physical presence. No tears, no emotion, yet just a focus and ever-loving fun like Crenshaw has never experienced on a golf course. A first-round, 2-under-par 70 develops the confidence needed to create a miracle.

"I didn't think mechanical thoughts," Crenshaw says. "That is when I play my best, when I play by instinct."

A pack of players near the lead entering Sunday dwindled to only Crenshaw, Davis Love III, and Greg Norman, as the usual back-nine battle at the Masters transpired. Love also carried a heavy heart. He too had learned lessons at the hand of Penick, the inspiration for Love's late father, teaching pro Davis Love Jr., who played collegiately for Penick at the University of Texas. On that Sunday when he died, one of Harvey's last acts was a couple of claps for Davis' victory at New Orleans, a win that earned a last-minute invitation to the Masters. Even Ben, as unconfident as he was about his golf game before the tournament began, had encouraged Davis to stay behind in Augusta and prepare for the Masters instead of traveling to Austin. Davis, he said, you're playing well, and Harvey would rather you honor him with your golf game.

Playing a few groups ahead of Crenshaw, Love finishes at 13-under par and waits in the nearby Jones Cabin for Ben to come home. That is when the buttery smooth putting stroke takes hold, again. Crenshaw converts a tricky, downhill five-footer for birdie on the par-3 sixteenth, then coaxes in a 13-footer for another birdie on the par-4 seventeenth. Two strokes clear of Love, Crenshaw prepares for his walk to glory. From the eighteenth tee on, Crenshaw is ready to crack.

"I lost concentration on my second shot to No. 18," Crenshaw says. "I was fortunate I had a two-shot lead."

This is where our picture is taken. Finally, his 274th shot of the week, a short putt for bogey, is holed on the left front portion of the eighteenth green. Crenshaw breaks down, bends at the waist, drops his head below his knees, grabs his face, inadvertently knocks off his white Buick cap, and sobs unashamedly. Look closely at Crenshaw's face and you can see the simultaneous grieving and rejoicing in one click of the camera. It could be a roaring laugh or a bawling cry. Crenshaw has won the Masters for a second, and most unlikely, time.

At arm's length is Jackson, approaching slowly from the middle of the green. The strength of the six-feet-four, 225-pound man is evident, but so is his gentle nature. A caddie of lesser knowledge and pedigree would be in full celebration, rushing up to lift Crenshaw off the ground with a bear hug or to revive him with jovial reminders that the Masters title is his. But here, instead, is a friend ready to comfort, approaching slowly, respecting the moment.

"Are you OK, are you all right?" Carl softly speaks. "How can I help?"

Crenshaw slowly lifts up his head, stands upright, and acknowledges Carl's question with a nod, then a brief hug into Carl's chest. The gallery's standing ovation peaks once again. No other words are necessary.

"I not only gave thanks to Carl, but also thanks because we were allowed to play well on that occasion," Crenshaw says today. "We had been close so many other times, and then this happened at this time. Unbelievable. All we needed to do was exchange a big, ol' hug."

This photograph is about more than just a player and his caddie, but two friends from very different backgrounds who have leaned on each other for more than a quarter century.

Ben Crenshaw *(left)* and Carl Jackson have worked together at the Masters Tournament since 1976, with the exception of 2000 when Carl was battling colon cancer. Carl still offers swing advice to Ben as he did here during a practice session at the 2003 Masters. (© *Augusta Chronicle*)

Crenshaw and Jackson form a partnership longer than any in Masters history, dating back to 1976. When Ben refers to Carl in interviews or his own writings, the word *friend* usually precedes the word *caddie.*

The years have been like an annual family reunion at Augusta National. Ben comes to town with friends and family in tow, in the role of the players' historian of Augusta National. Carl comes back home, either staying in a Washington Road hotel or with various friends in the area, reminiscing about his youth and caddies from a distant past. The player and caddie meet, talk about their families, trade rumors going through the sport, and then finally assess the current state of Ben's game and the plan for a week of golf at Augusta National. They chart their path around this familiar ground like a captain and his first mate crossing the same, but ever changing, course through the ocean. You can depend on their convergence like the heavy yellow of the pine pollen filtering down on a warm spring day in Augusta.

"Ben and I have a bond here that will never be broken," says Jackson, who was called simply 'Big Ol' Carl' by Crenshaw's late father, Charlie. "We are friends first, then player and caddie. That's unusual, I know, but that's why we have been together for so long."

To grasp the fulfillment that Jackson has experienced as a caddie and in his life, you must understand that he never knew anything but putting a golf bag over his shoulder and carrying it around the course. While many of his predecessors and associates developed "holes in their pockets," lost favor with their main players and wasted away because of alcohol abuse and other assorted maladies, Jackson took advantage of his good fortune to win two Masters titles with Crenshaw. He is not a wealthy man, but rich beyond monetary value, able to send four of his six children to college, and spend time with the younger two as they grow up.

Jackson was born in 1947, to a single mother, Margie Jackson, and raised in the Sand Hill neighborhood, up Berckmans Road from Augusta National, to the left and just beyond Wheeler Road before you reach Walton Way. Golf was a distant pastime to the black neighborhood boys in the 1950s, something that old, rich white men and out-of-towners came to Augusta to pursue. Carl's passion was baseball, just like many of his friends. His long, lanky frame and big feet positioned him to be quite an athlete.

That is where he developed a long-lost nickname "Skillet."

"I was a pitcher, at least I thought I was," Jackson says. "I wanted to be a major-league pitcher. Everybody I played with and against had the stuff to go to the majors. Some guys threw heat, BBs. But I just threw junk. I couldn't throw hard enough to break an egg. That's why they started calling me Skillet."

But the playgrounds did not bring home any money.

Raised in a "shotgun" house—"You could shoot a gun right through the front door all the way out the back without hitting anybody or anything," backdoor neighbor and caddie Tommy Bennett says—and facing the hard times of poverty, it was essential that everybody in the household contribute to put dinner on the table. Margie Jackson needed their help. By age eleven, word had passed down through the neighborhood that caddies at Augusta Country Club could earn a decent wage by simply carrying a golf bag around for a few hours. That is when guys like Jackson, Bennett, and Buck Moore began a lifelong journey. Jackson followed his older brother, Austin, nicknamed "Tweety," to Augusta Country Club and eventually earned another nickname, "Little Tweet," simply because the caddie master, "Big Henry" Avery, did not know Carl, but knew his older brother. Others jokingly also called him "Booger" because of a childhood habit of picking his nose. By 1959, twelve-year-old Carl Jackson had worked his way to Augusta National. What was first a weekend and summertime occupation had turned into a full-time job.

"You could make more money over there," Jackson says of Augusta National. "In 1960, I was a regular caddie at the National. Some of the caddies protested because here was this boy taking money out of their pockets. 'He should be in school,' they said. But some guys backed me, 'This kid needs money just as much as you do.' After that I fit right in with them.

"I was a good student in school, but unfortunately I had to quit school to help make a living for our family."

Jackson and his caddie mates also tried to play the sport, when they could find a break from the day's chores and sneak on the course.

"The only time we could get out there was after a big rain or something," Jackson recalls. "When all the members fled into the clubhouse, we would go out and play a few holes for as long as we could—until a guard came. Sometimes he'd shoot at us."

At first, the caddies thought the shots were just a scare tactic.

"We used to think he was shooting blanks," Jackson says, "until one day a bullet actually hit the tree I was standing behind. That was about it for me."

Jackson's first Masters bag was old-timer Billy Burke, the 1931 U.S. Open champion, in 1961. Only fourteen years old, Jackson probably thought he could beat Burke, who sported a white dress shirt and necktie for his rounds. Burke played in the first Masters in 1934, finishing a career-best third, and made 1961 his last Augusta start with rounds of 81-79. Burke earned $400, with only a small portion going to Jackson.

Jackson bounced from player to player as the years progressed, namely from Burke to Davis Love Jr., Gary Player, Tony Jacklin, Bruce Devlin, Steve Melnyk, Charlie Coe, R.H. Sikes, Mike Souchak, and Downing Gray before hooking up with Crenshaw. In 1964, the twenty-six-year-old Devlin was on the verge of returning to Australia to become a plumber because of a poor season, but worked with Jackson to finish fourth, earned $6,100, and stayed in the United States. His presence in the United States influenced other Australians, such as David Graham and Greg Norman, and today's crop of top players, to make Australia the largest producer of PGA Tour players outside of the United States. In 1971, the esteemed Ernest Nipper dropped Player's bag in the wake of threats and protests against Player and his native South Africa's apartheid policy. Jackson stepped in amid the possibility of protest and guided Player to a second-place finish.

Jackson's biggest early connection was not a Masters participant, but an Augusta National member. Arkansas billionaire Jackson T. Stephens, one of the nation's wealthiest men, would become the fourth chairman of Augusta National in 1991 and is currently the Chairman Emeritus. He took a liking to young Carl and hired him as his full-time caddie in 1962 when he joined Augusta National. He also persuaded Carl to leave his regular duties as an Augusta National caddie and move to Arkansas in the early 1970s to work for him in other capacities within his powerful financial business, Stephens Incorporated.

Stephens could understand Jackson's work ethic.

Stephens was a self-made man, working through the Depression by picking cotton and harvesting crops for neighbors and then, at age fifteen, becoming a bellhop, telegraph deliverer, and a shoeshine boy at night in Hope, Arkansas. Witt, his older brother, began the business during the 1930s and Jack joined in after World War II to transform it from a small Little Rock investment firm specializing in municipal bonds into Wall Street's fourth-largest investment bank and one of the largest financial empires in the South.

Stephens' company became closely associated in national business circles with Arkansans Sam Walton (Wal-Mart), William T. Dillard (Dillard's Department Store), and Dan Tyson (Tyson Foods). Jack and Witt were largely responsible for arranging some of the financing to launch Wal-Mart, Federal Express, and Tyson Foods.

Stephens joined Augusta National at age thirty-eight, just three years after taking up golf, and was a close associate of Augusta National's first chairman, Clifford Roberts, the co-founder of the club and the tournament with Bobby Jones. Stephens was very influential in political circles in his home state of Arkansas and in New York, where his business ties burgeoned. Many pay quiet respect to Stephens for being able to push the relatively unknown Arkansas Governor Bill Clinton from the backwoods of Little Rock into eight years in the White House in the 1990s. In many ways, Stephens is viewed as the quiet, thoughtful parallel to the often brazen, rough Roberts, who was a confidant and campaign influence to President Dwight D. Eisenhower in the 1950s and made sure that Ike became a quite public member of Augusta National in the late 1940s. Unlike the dictatorial presentation of Roberts and the easily accessible Hord Hardin, whom he succeeded as Augusta National chairman in 1991, Stephens was rarely available for comment on club or tournament issues and was not nearly as visible as his predecessors.

Stephens' status at Augusta National can be summed up by a physical presence on the grounds. Ten cabins that provide lodging for members and their guests are bunched just to the left of the tenth hole. Two of the most prominent are the Eisenhower Cabin, more affectionately called Mamie's Cabin, after the former president's wife; and the Jones Cabin, named after the esteemed Mr. Jones, both of which rest just to the left of the tenth tee. The Butler Cabin, set just beyond the putting green, has had its basement used as the studio home of CBS's televised green jacket ceremony since 1964. Behind these three prominent structures, set in a semicircle just to the right as you walk to the Par-3 Course, are seven more cabins named after various members. The last one built, in 1969, with a noticeably large back porch, is the Stephens Cabin.

Stephens' mark is evident elsewhere here. Augusta National's first black member, Ron Townsend, joined in 1991, just as Stephens was taking over the leadership role. It was Stephens who investigated building a golf facility for children after Tiger Woods won the 1997 Masters and then donated $5 million of his own money to The First Tee, a golf industry-wide initiative to provide access to the sport for underprivileged youth, when the program was unveiled in 1997. Two First Tee facilities are open in Arkansas today. Stephens' influence on that agenda created Augusta National's public donation and partnership with the same program.

Officially, Carl worked in records and promotions for the Independent Corporation of America in Little Rock, but predominantly Stephens relied upon Carl as his right-hand man, whether it be caddying at Augusta National, entertaining at the Stephens Cabin, or on business trips. "He never went into another store to shop after I moved there, I can tell you that," Carl says. Carl remembers one Arkansas newspaper in the early 1970s that referred to him as Stephens' "haughte," a term that could have been translated as racially derogatory but more than likely meant Carl was as close an associate as any Stephens had.

Stephens comes off as a good ol' boy at first glance. He is slow speaking, Southern, and ponders most questions with a long pause and a drag from a cigarette. However, his business acumen and dry sense of humor reveal a highly intelligent man.

Stephens trusted Carl with classified information and

wanted him within earshot when important conversations took place.

"I knew his innermost thoughts," Jackson says. "I was always by his side. If he had too much to drink and somebody called on the telephone, he made sure I was on the other phone to make sure exactly what was said. The only time he was vulnerable was when he was drinking."

Jackson remembers an early 1980s business meeting in Palm Beach, Florida, with Jack Nicklaus. Normally low key about displaying his wealth, for some reason Stephens opted to drive his Rolls Royce to the meeting with Nicklaus. Usually, this type of face-to-face meeting occurred with just Stephens and the other party talking behind closed doors. But not on this occasion.

"When they greeted each other at (Nicklaus') office, I said excuse me," Jackson says. "But Mr. Stephens said, 'No Carl, I want you to stay.' That sort of surprised Jack a little bit. Then the three of us sat down. I guess Mr. Stephens figured I was an important part of that conversation."

Jimmy Carter, the thirty-ninth president of the United States, was a roommate of Stephens in the U.S. Naval Academy just after World War II. When the Georgia governor was campaigning for the 1976 Presidential election, he stayed not only in the Stephens' house, but bumped Jackson out of his room.

Stephens' children, five and ten years younger than Carl, grew close to him as they grew up. Warren A. Stephens, the younger brother, eventually also became an Augusta National member.

"We were definitely like family there," Carl says. "They always said I was their black brother."

By 1990, that relationship had soured. Carl had married for a third time—his first wife died and he divorced from his second wife—and he wanted to spend more time with new wife Debra, their two children apiece from previous marriages, and their two young children together, Jason and Carlisa. Stephens wanted him alongside on various trips. Finally, Carl decided it was time to break loose, leave the employment of

Stephens, and depart Arkansas after more than twenty-five years there. It was a bitter parting. The two did not talk for years.

"My kids come before anybody," Carl says. "After what I went through as a kid, I wanted to be there for my family, not away somewhere else."

Too bad they could not patch up their differences, because Carl's largely uneventful Masters weeks toiling for player after player ended thanks to Stephens.

Following the 1975 Masters, Crenshaw was searching for another caddie from the home club. When Ben made his Masters debut as an amateur in 1972, the first caddie he met when he walked onto the grounds and stopped by the caddie shack was Willie "Cemetery" Perteet, the longtime caddie for former President Eisenhower. Eventually, Crenshaw was assigned a caddie simply known as Luke, whom he described as "a great, funny man."

But Luke was not the answer for a promising player such as Crenshaw. The three-time NCAA Championship winner needed a steady hand to bridle his wild game. During one of the first years playing in the Masters, Crenshaw faced a long second shot into the par-4 fifth hole. Luke suggested a 5-iron; Crenshaw thought it was a 4-iron.

"Luke, I'm not sure I can quite get there with a 5," Crenshaw said in his usual aw-shucks demeanor.

"Well, hit the 4-iron then," Luke shot back fiercely with a frown on his face.

Crenshaw needed more understanding than that. In his first four Masters appearances, he made the cut every time, twice as an amateur, but failed to contend. As Crenshaw prepared for the 1976 Masters, his third Augusta start as a professional, he was seeking more guidance. John Griffith, an Augusta National member and Crenshaw family friend from Fort Worth, Texas, referred Ben to Jackson after Stephens heard about the search. They talked with Freddie Bennett, the caddie master, to work out the details. And, as they say, it was the beginning of a beautiful relationship.

The first year together, Crenshaw may have finished eight

shots behind the record-setting Raymond Floyd, but he was in second place. Over their first twenty years together, Crenshaw recorded two wins, eleven top-ten finishes, and missed only two cuts.

"It was just incredible how well Carl knew the greens," Crenshaw says. "He thought his way around like a player, which I really appreciated. He has great imagination. It was very strange also because he very seldom relied on yardages. We were a team right from the start."

Perhaps even more important was the sense that these two were meant for each other on this hallowed ground. When Crenshaw won his first Masters in 1984, he was in the middle of a divorce from his first wife, Polly. Much like 1995, Carl took the focus of the week and placed it solely on the golf course.

"He brought the golf out of me," Crenshaw remembers. "He started the week by saying let's work real hard on the little approach shots, the kind of thing you can overlook at Augusta National. When you play in the Masters, your first priority is to drive the ball the best you can. But as we went through the practice rounds that week, Carl just guided me around. He'd say, 'Hit the ball from here. Take an approach putt from here because the pin is gonna be here this week.' Carl is so good at that. He got my mind ready to play, to the point where I didn't feel the suddenness you sometimes feel when the Masters starts on Thursday. My long game and short game were in sync."

When the back nine came on Sunday, Crenshaw drained a memorable 60-foot birdie putt on the par-4 tenth hole, his third consecutive birdie, only to turn around and bogey the eleventh. As they stood on the tee of the treacherous par-3 twelfth hole, Crenshaw was the leader. And in his ear was Jackson. They picked a 6-iron.

"Don't worry about that bogey," Jackson whispered before Ben addressed his tee shot. "You're playing well. We'll get through this thing."

A subsequent birdie on the twelfth secured his lead and Crenshaw went on to capture his first green jacket.

"I was reading an article in a magazine where they talked about the ghosts out there that year," Jackson said. "There was something special going on that week. I'm going to tell Ben it wasn't ghosts, it was angels. We just sort of knew it was going to happen."

Their teamwork was awe-inspiring to many of Crenshaw's competitors.

"There's a guy (Jackson) that can read those greens," Nick Price said in 1989. "I have the greatest admiration for that man. There aren't too many that know the greens as well as he does. When you have two brains like that working together that's why Ben holes so many putts. I remember what he did (in 1988) in one round here with his putter. In the first seven holes, Ben hit one green and was 1-under par."

The Masters relationship expanded to the PGA Tour in the early 1990s. Carl was on Ben's bag when he won a second Southwestern Bell Colonial at Fort Worth in 1990. He stayed on in 1991. But the stress of being away from family, coupled with the absence of that Augusta magic, put an end to the weekly association. Carl's green-reading did not have the same local knowledge effect at places such as Riviera or Doral as it did at Augusta.

Still, the link with Crenshaw enabled Jackson to take routes in life he would never have previously considered. Rumor has it, and Carl will not confirm it, but the 1995 caddie payday from Crenshaw far exceeded the usual ten percent and a fat tip for the winning caddie. Some say it soared to nearly $90,000. "Let's just say that Ben did me right," Carl says. In the late 1990s, Carl partnered in a golf company, Diamondized Golf, that developed specialty wedges. Carl was titled Director of Tour Operations and moved to Atlanta. Even though the venture was not successful, it allowed Carl to spread his wings.

Carl and his family moved to the mountains of North Carolina in 1999, first to Hendersonville and now on to Asheville. Jason is fifteen, tall and rangy just like his father some forty years ago, and a budding star in football as a tight end and one of the leading tacklers as outside linebacker for the Asheville T.C. Roberson High Rams. He also excels off the field, being recommended for Honors classes and participating in ROTC. Both young children are excellent students and college bound. They follow in the footsteps of the older half-brothers and sisters, all of whom are college graduates or working toward that end. Carrethia, the oldest child at age 35, attended the University of Arkansas and now lives in Silver Springs, Maryland. Carl Romeo, the oldest boy, attended Clark-Atlanta University on an academic scholarship. Jonitha attended the University of Arkansas–Little Rock. Crystal attends the University of St. Louis on a scholarship. Not a bad record for Carl, who barely made it to high school.

Debra, also an Augusta native, was spending the week two hours away in Charlotte as a student nurse and in pursuit of her master's degree at the University of North Carolina at Charlotte. But in 2003 she worked out an arrangement to be closer to the family in Asheville. Carl spends his little bit of free time studying herbal medicine or caddying.

Carl wishes that caddying would be a distant second, except for the spring trek home. Carl will occasionally depart for a few weeks at a time. He used to cruise down to Durham, pick up Bennett, and drive around the eastern part of the country, to a succession of PGA Tour or Nationwide Tour events, looking for a green player or a grizzled veteran to latch onto. Usually it is a different player every week. But that road gets old real fast. Coming back from the John Deere Classic in the summer of 2002, Carl's car broke down in Tennessee and he was forced to get it towed home and then purchase a new vehicle.

In 2003, Crenshaw came looking for a little more of that magic. Since turning fifty in early 2002, his golf game has all but deserted him. Inconsistent ball striking combined with an unsteady short game had made Crenshaw lose interest. His golf course design business was critically acclaimed and thriving. His three daughters, ages 5, 11, and 15, were pulling for Daddy to come home. However, Ben could not stomach ending his playing days on such a sour note.

Therefore, at the 2003 Masters, he dropped the question to Carl again.

"I'm struggling," Crenshaw uttered. "Come help me out for a while. Then we'll sit down and talk."

"I'm there," Carl came back.

From the Liberty Mutual Legends of Golf in mid-April at Savannah, Georgia, through the U.S. Senior Open in late June at Inverness in Toledo, Ohio, they were a week-to-week team again. They would go to the practice area after another bad round, with Ben working on his swing and Carl standing by to offer tidbits of advice. Only this time, it did not work out as well. Ben broke 70 only twice in sixteen rounds, made just over $54,000, and had a high finish of twentieth at the Bruno's Memorial Classic in Birmingham, Alabama. Consecutive 77-79 starts and missed cuts at the Senior PGA Championship and U.S. Senior Open made the sitdown with Jackson a parting of the ways. Ben realized his game was not up to speed at the moment and Carl, quite frankly, needed more money to last on the road.

So, in July, Carl took off from Asheville for his trip to the Northeast again, this time on a lonely sojourn since Bennett had moved from Durham. Carl went to the B.C. Open and Greater Hartford Open looking for a bag, worked for two weeks, and then circled back to Asheville.

He and Crenshaw insist that they will continue to team at Augusta until one of them cannot go any longer. Carl insists that he would not make a sudden move to a young Masters hopeful, such as a Charles Howell III, unless Ben gave his total, unsolicited blessing.

Mostly, the Carl Jackson of today is "Mr. Mom" at home in Asheville, making sure the children do not spend too much time on the phone, hovering over their school lessons, or proudly attending football games. That is not too far from the MO for Crenshaw.

"I am the lowest of the low in this household," Jackson says with a laugh. "We've got two computers in this home. We're busy all the time, going here and there. The expenses build up. But that's a good sign of the times. All my kids are doing well in school. That's my commitment in life."

Life is something that Jackson cherishes because he is simply here. In February 2000, he was diagnosed with colon cancer, the second-most common cause of cancer death in the United States. He was so weak after chemotherapy treatments early that year that he told Crenshaw to find a replacement. Their twenty-fifth anniversary pairing at the Masters would have to wait. Linn Strickler, Crenshaw's regular Tour caddie, stepped in. The signs were not good. Colon cancer is treatable if discovered in its early stages, but when it spreads to other organs, the survival rate lessens, especially for a man in his early fifties. Caddies, tournament officials, and players called and sent their best wishes.

"I walked in to see the doctor and he told me I needed immediate surgery," Jackson says. "When he said I've got colon cancer, I just prayed about it."

Crenshaw prayed too because he knows illness. In 1985, he mysteriously lost thirty pounds. Doctors diagnosed him with hyperthyroidism and prescribed four months' worth of radioactive iodine treatments, which gradually got his condition under control. Crenshaw was so concerned about Carl's condition that he called him every day at one point, especially when the Masters date closed in. He offered financial assistance. You could almost hear the tears pouring over the telephone into Jackson's hospital room.

"Hey, you take care of your own business," Crenshaw said. "Those doctors there know what it is. Tell them to go ahead and fix it."

"That was a great lift," Jackson says. "When Ben tells you something, he means it."

Jackson credits his doctor and the use of liquid oxygen for his recovery. "I feel better than ever, like I was never sick," he said in 2001. Today, he gladly goes to local charity golf tournaments when invited, proudly professing to be a cancer survivor.

He also points out the role that herbal medicine played in his healing. Jackson first heard of alternative medical care more

Carl Jackson has been a caddie his entire life, beginning as a preteen at Augusta Country Club, as a regular at the Augusta National Golf Club, and in the Masters Tournament and on the PGA Tour and Champions Tour. His main goal is to provide for his family, which includes two school-age children at home in Asheville, North Carolina. (© *Augusta Chronicle*)

than twenty years ago when he traveled from his home in Arkansas to a religious rally held by Tennessee pastor Mamon Wilson. He watched as Wilson magically worked an inoperable baseball-sized tumor lodged in a man's mouth out the side of his face with only the slightest bit of damage. He heard of other "healings" where people with tumors were treated and miraculously survived. In 2002, Jackson spent hours in classes studying herbal medicine and continues to pursue avenues to get some of the medication into the marketplace. He is as passionate about this effort as he is stalking a ten-foot putt at Augusta National.

As Jackson pursued his family and religious beliefs, Crenshaw was inducted into the World Golf Hall of Fame in mid-November 2002. It was an honor particularly poignant because Penick was enshrined at the same time during ceremonies in St. Augustine, Florida.

Not to be lost in this ceremony was Crenshaw's Hall of Fame collection of memorabilia that was on display during and after his induction. It included a replica of "Little Ben," a Masters green jacket, and right there in the middle, the Masters caddie jumpsuit that Carl Jackson wore when Ben won in 1995.

Surely, somebody will take a picture of that. It is a worthy addition to the Crenshaw-Jackson collection.

Tiger's First Caddie: Burnt Biscuits

Tommy Bennett is talking on his cellular phone, in between shots on the golf course, playing his own game in the Tidewater area of Virginia. Only hours before, one of his most recent bags on the PGA Tour, New Zealand's Michael Long, missed the cut in the 2002 Michelob Championship at Kingsmill.

"I had to play, just had to," says Bennett. "It's in my blood."

It was just another day on the PGA Tour for the fifty-four-year-old Bennett, an Augusta native and former Augusta National Golf Club caddie. For most of his caddying career, Bennett has gone from bag to bag, crisscrossing the country by car on different Tours to try and find a steady paycheck. He estimates that he has toted for more than fifty players, beginning in the 1969 Atlanta Classic when Allan Henning earned $184 for a seventy-second-place finish. His longest tenure came in the late 1990s when he worked with Tom Pernice Jr. for just over two years. Bennett has never won on a Tour bag, with a best Masters finish of fourth in 1987 working for Jodie Mudd, and a handful of seconds in other Tour events. Jobs seem to last as long as under-par scores and a prompt arrival at the golf course. He is the poster boy for the caddie on Tour—a gypsy.

Nevertheless, Bennett holds one claim to fame. He was

Tiger Woods' first Masters Tournament caddie. That came in Tiger's 1995 Masters debut when the raw, nineteen-year-old reigning U.S. Amateur champion and Stanford University freshman made headlines at Augusta National.

And just think: Bennett did not want Tiger's bag.

Bennett hoped to work with Dicky Pride, an up-and-coming twenty-five-year old Alabaman who had won his first PGA Tour event the previous year as a rookie in the FedEx St. Jude Classic at Memphis. A good Masters showing by Pride would mean a nice paycheck, while Woods' ability to ante up and also make the cut was debatable.

"I wanted to caddie for the Masters champion, and I figured Dicky Pride had a better shot than Tiger Woods, the amateur," Bennett says. "But Jack Stephens (the former Augusta National chairman) said he wished I would caddie for Tiger in the Masters. That made it a done deal."

Tiger Woods, then a first-time amateur participant in the Masters, and caddie Tommy "Burnt Biscuits" Bennett, walk to the ninth green in the 1995 Masters. Bennett was Woods' first Masters caddie. (© *Augusta Chronicle*)

Bennett was picked to loop for Woods during the practice rounds for the 1995 Masters "because I was the only caddie on hand with PGA Tour experience and local knowledge," he says. Still, Tiger wished that his mentor and father, Earl Woods, would tote for him. The occasion called for such an appearance. The nation's black population, whether golfers or not, was watching, as were the caddies at Augusta National. Tiger was the first black amateur in the field. Tiger pointed out that he often had friends or family caddie for him; witness the victory in the 1994 U.S. Amateur at the Tournament Players Club at Sawgrass in Ponte Vedra Beach, Florida, when Navy Capt. Jay Brunza, a sports psychologist and family friend, was on the bag.

Bennett was selected to tutor Tiger in the 1995 Masters practice rounds and then step aside. He carried thirty-six holes on Monday of Masters Week, in a group with Nick Faldo in the morning and Trip Kuehne, the 1994 U.S. Amateur runner-up, in the afternoon. Raymond Floyd, Greg Norman, Fred Couples, Nick Price, and Gary Player also joined Woods during practice rounds on Tuesday and Wednesday and during the Par-3 Contest. They wanted a glimpse of what they would have to overcome in the future. Lee Elder, a special invitee twenty years after breaking the player color barrier at the Masters, made a special effort to speak with Tiger and follow just about every shot.

But questions arose about Earl's on-course role as the tournament grew closer. Was he physically capable of this task? Butch Harmon, Tiger's instructor, was not sure. Other observers echoed Elder, "I think it's a mistake."

The usually self-confident Earl seemed ready ... to a point.

"We have an excellent relationship," Earl said of his son. "I know how to interface with Tiger. Most fathers couldn't do it because you have to have a role reversal. He's the boss. You are nothing but a peon out there. Most fathers couldn't make that transition. With us, it's no problem.

"I don't know how a sixty-two-year-old is going to handle those hills down there. I don't think I'm going to like that white uniform. It looks hot just to look at it."

On Tuesday night, Tiger and Company decided that Bennett would be the man for the week. Bennett said they did not let him know he would carry in the tournament until Wednesday afternoon's Par-3 Contest was completed.

"I really didn't have a job until then," Bennett says. "It was all evaluation until they told me to get ready for Thursday."

Lucky for Bennett, as Pride would shoot 79-73–152 to miss the cut by seven strokes. To date, that has been Pride's only Masters appearance.

Bennett's most lasting impression of Tiger occurred on the first tee Thursday morning. It was a rainy, cool first day of play. Paired with defending champion José Maria Olazabal and with nearly the entire Masters gallery craning their necks to watch this new phenomenon, Tiger walked to the first tee, sporting his Stanford cap, shook hands with the Augusta National members who serve as starters, and mentally prepared to tee off. To the right of the tee box, Bennett was getting set also. He counted clubs, checked his yardage book, and then bent down to the ball pocket of Woods' small carry bag to retrieve a ball. He searched quickly in the pocket of the bag and swallowed hard. His eyes got big as he sidestepped over to Tiger.

"We've only got three balls in here," Tommy quietly and incredulously told Tiger as he prepared to hand over the driver.

"We've got three balls; that's all I need," Woods said straight-faced.

"I just thought, 'Man, you're at Augusta National in the Masters for the first time. Whew, who you kidding?' " Bennett says. "But that's all we took onto the golf course all week, three balls, no more, no less. He was that confident, even then."

Bennett says that Woods listened to his advice about the golf course, but that he was his own man, soaking in the atmosphere and the precision necessary to play Augusta National. Every morning, Bennett would meet Harmon at the driving range, just before Tiger warmed up, and Harmon would dole out some simple instructions for the day.

"He was an easy man to work for; anybody could work for

Tiger," Bennett says. "Tiger knew what he could do on the golf course. But when he came to the Masters, he didn't know anything about this golf course. He learned pretty fast."

Tiger dazzled the crowd with his prodigious length off the tee, hitting no more than an 8-iron into the 500-yard par-5 fifteenth every day and no more than a 7-iron all week into any of the par 4s. In Friday's second round, Bennett recalls Woods' second shot from 232 yards (250 to the hole) on the par-5 thirteenth hole. From a sidehill lie in the right trees, Woods cut a 3-iron into the green to within fifteen feet and two-putted for birdie.

But Tiger struggled with distance control on his irons, blowing the ball over a few greens and spinning it off the front on others, and shot three even-par rounds of 72 and a third-round 77 on the way to a tie for forty-first. He had the usual rookie embarrassments, beginning with a thirty-foot birdie putt on the first green in the first round that rolled off the green and down a slope on the left side, some fifty feet away from the hole.

Still, he won Low Amateur honors and made a statement that Augusta National was a course he could overpower. Tiger averaged 311.1 yards per drive, No. 1 in the tournament, and nearly five yards more than the second-place finisher in driving distance, Davis Love III.

"That's where all this talk about changing the golf course at Augusta National began," says Bennett, pointing to the addition of more than 350 yards from 2001 to 2003. "They rebuilt the golf course because of what they saw coming at them that year. There's no doubt about that.

"See, that's why they called him Tiger. Because he was going to be feared."

Woods made a point to connect with the mostly black Augusta National employees, particularly the caddies, that week. He signed autographs daily as he walked under the large oak trees behind the clubhouse, in the clubhouse, at the bag storage area on the north end of the clubhouse, and around the driving range entrance. He invited Bennett up to the Crow's Nest, the traditional amateur quarters at the top of the clubhouse, for a hamburger after one round. It was Bennett's first trip there.

After making the cut on Friday, Tiger, Earl, Bennett, and Brunza hopped in a car and drove twenty minutes over to Forest Hills Golf Club, one of the city's best and most historic public courses. Tiger put on a clinic for junior golfers and caddies at dinnertime on a driving range tee nearly devoid of grass. About twenty caddies with Augusta National ties were on hand to watch Tiger show his stuff, particularly a hilarious act where he zoomed 3-irons over Earl's head as the elder Woods casually stood about twenty yards away serving as the emcee. Afterward, Bennett served as a tour guide as the foursome drove through Bennett's old Sand Hill neighborhood up above Augusta National where "we just visualized how things used to be."

"Just knowing that Tiger came to hit balls for them is enough to get some of these kids playing golf," said former caddie Jariah Beard. "As for the caddies, we deeply appreciated it. We have been the forgotten men of the Masters, but maybe Tiger will help us be remembered."

For Bennett, a cousin of longtime Augusta National caddie master Freddie Bennett, the experience was unforgettable. It was one of the last times he would caddie at Augusta National and his last Masters appearance. By 1997, a year after Caddie Master Enterprises took over the Augusta National caddie corps, Bennett was gone, he says, because "they didn't like my attitude." He was not cast to follow in the footsteps of boyhood neighbor Carl Jackson, who has served a long courtship with Ben Crenshaw. By 1996, Brunza was on Woods' bag at the Masters. Then for the historic victory in 1997 in his professional debut, Mike "Fluff" Cowan had been hired to work with Woods. Woods' next two Masters were won with Steve Williams on the bag. Bennett did get a picture in *Sports Illustrated* in 1995 with his five-year-old son Donte and Woods. And Earl forked over "a pretty decent" $1,500 for the week's caddie fee. Plus, a large, fading mural still adorns the wall of the Sand Hill Grill in his old neighborhood, depicting Bennett carrying Woods' bag in 1995.

"Oh, I still see him around," Bennett says of Woods. "I'll speak to him sometime. But he's in another world now."

Bennett trudges on in a career that came to him because "it was our lunch money for the week." He and Jackson lived in back-to-back shotgun houses when they were growing up, playing baseball and caddying at Augusta Country Club and Augusta National by the early 1960s, working at the hand of legendary Willie "Pappy" Stokes. Bennett worked hard to make it to the level where he could caddie in the tournament.

"If there were 100 caddies at Augusta National, I sure didn't want to be No. 100," Bennett says.

Bennett owns one of the most unusual nicknames, "Burnt Biscuits," among Augusta National caddies. It has nothing to do with his caddying skills, but came about when he tried to sneak through a window at his grandmother's house to confiscate some freshly baked biscuits. Upon jumping out the window when his grandmother came running, Tommy kicked a pot of boiling water off the wood-burning stove, started a house fire, and burned his legs.

He lived in Durham, North Carolina, for most of the late 1990s and early 2000s after meeting a woman from that central Tar Heel state city. She was vacationing in Hawaii while Tommy was looping at the Hawaiian Open. Bennett played casual rounds of golf at Hillandale Golf Course, the city-owned municipal course, with "a few hustlers." Bennett and Jackson, who lives about four hours west in Asheville, would car pool to tournaments, staying on the road for as much as a month, trying to find a hot bag that was available.

Bennett has had a few big opportunities in his Tour caddying over the past three years, then watched it wash away. Augusta native Charles Howell III hired him at the end of the 2001 season for a handful of events. He also worked for Matt Kuchar for a few events in 2001 when Kuchar earned his Tour card for 2002. Neither relationship with very promising young players lasted very long. Bennett was tardy a few times and put the nail in his coffin by asking Howell if he could borrow money on the first tee the night after a cash deficit in a casino during the Las Vegas stop.

"I've lost a few dollars there," Bennett says of Vegas. "All the caddies go through that in Vegas. You can win some and lose some. Every time I go there, I lose some."

Today, Bennett is still on the run. He left Durham following a breakup with his girlfriend in 2002 and spent a few days in an Atlanta jail for driving without a license, according to Jackson. Following the Tour as a caddie was his way of life. Bennett still believes he will find a steady bag, but it will not be because he is an Augusta National caddie.

"I couldn't work there again," Bennett says. "There are too many memories there. That walk down memory lane would be tough."

The Place

The Caddie Master

Freddie Bennett never had to travel very far to reach another world. It was in his backyard.

He was practically born on the golf course in 1930, growing up just off the sixteenth fairway at Augusta Country Club in an area called "The Sand Hill." Freddie swam in Rae's Creek as a child, right in front of the twelfth green, and remembers the cows grazing on the Augusta National grounds during World War II. When it came time to retire as the caddie master at the Augusta National Golf Club in 2000, all he had to do was mosey a mile or so away, to his current home located a block above a cemetery and three blocks from Berckmans Road. In between, he made a name for himself for more than fifty years as a caddie and, more prominently, caddie master.

During a forty-one-year caddie master reign at Augusta National, the only name you had to call to make something happen was Freddie. "I went to see Freddie," is the ringing endorsement many Masters participants uttered when they needed a change of caddies or advice about hiring a caddie. He paired most of the Augusta National caddies with the players and members. Some duos became long-term relationships,

Freddie Bennett *(right)*, the Augusta National caddie master, goes over a scorecard with Ernest Nipper, Gary Player's caddie, during the 1968 Masters. Bennett wore a uniform to display his rank. He was responsible for pairing many of the top player-caddie teams in Masters history during the 1960s and 1970s. (© *Augusta Chronicle*)

others simply year-to-year or day-to-day partnerships. He recruited extra caddies for the tournament or for member play by occasionally driving his station wagon into various Augusta neighborhoods and transporting potential caddies back to the Washington Road course. He had a backup plan if a caddie had to be fired or did not show up, helped store the players' golf gear, laundered the famous caddie jumpsuits (five sets of 100 uniforms at one time in the late 1960s), found some minor medication for players' queasy stomachs, and, in a pinch, could even repair a player's broken equipment. In other words, he did everything, all on a flat salary with no commission.

"I love it, but I'm getting steadily gray, got an ulcer and it is a worrisome job that'll just get tougher because caddies are disappearing," Bennett, then age thirty-seven, said in 1968.

In the later years of his Masters duty, he could often be found perched atop a stool in the bag room that sits attached to the clubhouse near the first fairway. He greeted players, caddies, Augusta National members, and various international officials. The roster of celebrities he greeted included Presidents Eisenhower, Nixon, Ford, Reagan, and Bush, Bob Hope, and Michael Jordan.

Freddie had a gruff exterior and booming, baritone voice that could rattle even the most experienced caddie.

"Freddie's a nice guy," says Edward White, who remains today as the club's man in charge of the bag room and cart fleet. "He's got his ways. When he acts like he's mad, he's just trying to throw you off. He gets steamed up every now and then. But with Freddie, today is today and tomorrow is tomorrow."

Bennett came about his job by being in the right spot at the right time.

He was a caddie at heart, first serving in the Masters as a sixteen-year old in 1946, toting for Billy Burke. Jackie Burke Jr., Frank Stranahan, Peter Thomson, Jay Hebert, and Chick Evans would follow.

Stranahan's story is particularly memorable. The wealthy amateur, who was one of the first golfers to train with weights, was playing a Masters practice round in 1948 when he had a verbal confrontation with the Augusta National superintendent Marion Luke. It seemed Stranahan was playing more than one ball in his practice rounds, chipping and putting excessively to learn all the nuances of the course. Playing more than one ball was forbidden in those days and still is; just notice the small signs on the first and tenth tees during the practice rounds that state, "One ball only." However, tournament officials put up with it as long as the player does not abuse the policy and play a bucket of balls on each hole.

But Stranahan kept on and on during a particularly wet day at Augusta National. Finally, Augusta National officials asked him to leave the course on the eighth green. He had been disqualified after some of the members monitored Stranahan's actions.

"He said, 'I only hit two balls,'" Bennett remembers. "There were balls all over the green, but Frank didn't explain they

Freddie Bennett, the longtime caddie master at Augusta National, poses at his post near the bag room in the clubhouse in 2000. The alley way to the left leads to the first fairway. Bennett retired at Augusta National in 2000 after more than forty years as a caddie and caddie master. (© *Augusta Chronicle*)

were there for putting. On No. 6, he asked me if they were still following him. I told him they were. When he got to No. 8, they said, 'Get off the course.' "

John Henry "Eleven" Williams was Bennett's predecessor as caddie master at Augusta National. He became a caddie as a youngster and took the caddie corps after World War II. Eleven sported a uniform that resembled an old-fashioned cab driver, complete with a large cap, and gave many of the caddies of the 1940s and 1950s their nicknames. He was also known as an excellent club repairman.

Bennett served in the military for two years in the late 1940s and then took a bricklayers' course. After laying bricks for a couple years, Bennett figured his passion was working at Augusta National. He came back to the club in the early 1950s to work on the maintenance crew.

Williams died suddenly on October 16, 1959, at age forty-five, suffering a cerebral hemorrhage while working during the Augusta National off-season at The Broodmoor Club in Colorado Springs, Colorado, for former Augusta National head professional Ed Dudley. Bennett, in his late twenties, was quickly named Augusta National caddie master just as the club opened for the 1959–60 season. It was a time when Eisenhower was in office, Arnold Palmer was becoming "The King," and Jack Nicklaus was a rotund young amateur.

His position running the caddie corps at Augusta National came with high prestige. Billy Ricks, a former Augusta National caddie, said when the group would hit a bar downtown after a long day caddying, they would invite the caddie master along. In their minds, buying him a beer would be a good way to try to get an angle on a bag for the next day.

"The caddie master never bought a drink, no sir," Ricks says. "Hey, but that didn't necessarily mean you'd get a bag either."

The caddie master's most arduous task was assigning caddies for players or members. In the old days, your caddie IQ got you a long way. Bennett knew his men's strengths. If a player needed particular help with club selection, Bennett might choose Ernest Nipper, a good player and yardage man, to work the bag. A player yearning for some help on Augusta National's difficult greens might get Matthew "Shorty Mac" Palmer, renowned for his keen sense for reading greens. Looking for a reliable, steady hand who could work with anyone? How about Joe Collins. For members, meshing personalities was just as important as caddying ability. The player had to know where to go and when and also how to interact with the member.

John Henry "Eleven" Williams was the original caddie master at Augusta National, serving that role from the mid-1940s until his death in 1959. Williams earned his nickname because 11 was the number he wore as a caddie before becoming the caddie master. He was famous for his patented caddie master uniform and an ability to repair clubs. (© Historic Golf Photos/Ron Watts Collection)

Bennett recognized his best caddies by offering them the best player bags or the highest-paying members' clubs. One way that you could tell his best caddies was by the wear and tear on their "tenni-pumps." Bennett estimated that a good caddie would wear out approximately forty pairs of shoes during a season, which lasted from the club's opening in mid-October until late May.

Bennett worked with a crew of thirty-five to forty caddies most of the year. Having a car was a luxury for many of the caddies, and 8 A.M. was the magic time where the first-come, first-served policy rewarded the drivers who could pull into the parking lot before the other caddies who were forced to ride the 8 A.M. Augusta city bus that dumped them at the entrance to Augusta National. On many occasions, caddies for member play made their mark beginning on Friday afternoon when they would be assigned to a member's party that arrived for either nine or eighteen holes, which carried over to multiple rounds on Saturday and a concluding eighteen holes on Sunday morning if the player-caddie relationship worked. The number of caddies at least doubled with part-timers coming on in the weeks leading up to the Masters in hopes of becoming famous in the tournament. School-age boys would volunteer to caddie just that week at no charge. Bennett watched out for his yearlong regulars by making sure they received first dibs on a Masters bag.

In the late 1960s, caddie fees for member play were $3 for nine holes and $6 for eighteen. That has increased to a minimum of $55 per bag today, with most usually making at least $75 with tips during normal days and sometimes much more. In the late 1960s, a Masters caddie fee was $10 per day but most made at least $100 for the tournament. Today's Masters winning caddie can earn as much as $100,000 with the usual ten percent cut.

In 1968, Bennett described the caddie selection process for the Masters: "Julius Boros' caddie of last year, Henry Jenkins, got a little old, so we gave him a job sticking decals and gave Boros Rufus Whitfield. See, we try to give the new, good players our best available and our best available try to get the good players. They can read, they know who they are."

When one caddie was picked for a group of member play, that caddie had the option of picking three more to join his foursome, creating an atmosphere of camaraderie and tutoring. When Caddie Master Enterprises took over operation of the caddies in 1996, the caddie system became a lottery. Each caddie had his own number, which was drawn out of a bag. Each caddie in the foursome was chosen by this drawing instead of the previous system by which the fit caddies survived. There were some favorites played by the members, but no one was guaranteed a day's work, even though the basic benefits improved.

"I think it was good for the caddies because they had a salary," Bennett says. "They may not have made quite as much money. But they could go on unemployment in the summer when the course was closed (from May until October)."

Being the caddie master also fostered unusual relationships. Augusta National cofounder and original club chairman Clifford Roberts persuaded Bennett to take part in a comical club film one year in the early 1970s, to be shown during the members' annual early spring Jamboree weekend. The film portrayed a bear running all over the grounds at Augusta National, stealing clubs and causing havoc. The man inside the suit was Bennett, even though the conclusion of the film revealed that it was supposed to be Roberts.

When Roberts committed suicide on the grounds in 1977, Bennett had theories about what happened. He remembered Roberts coming on the club grounds for that particular visit with fresh $100 bills in his wallet and the chairman was empty-pocketed when his body was discovered near Ike's Pond on the Par-3 Course. Bennett contends that Roberts was too frail and it was too dark that night for him to walk down to the Par-3 Course. He thinks Roberts paid an overnight guard to drive him to the short course and then drop him off. Roberts was discovered with a fatal bullet wound to the head.

Bennett's life today is far removed from the fast pace at Augusta National. He is a persistent visitor with old friends in the Sand Hill area, sitting on a porch early in the morning or getting a cup of coffee at a neighborhood restaurant. He will occasionally go fishing, a longtime passion.

His retirement in 2000 was coming on in 1996 when Caddie Master Enterprises took over. That took all of the responsibility of choosing caddies out of Bennett's hands. Tom Van Dorn was brought in by the caddie corporation to run the show, leaving Bennett hanging out at the end of the clubhouse to talk about the old times when he ran the show at Augusta National.

"I won't be here," Bennett said in 2000 about coming back to Augusta National (even though he does visit). "I'm gone. That's it. I won't be back. I've seen enough."

Top 10

When Freddie Bennett retired as caddie master at Augusta National in 2000, he provided his top-10 list of the top Augusta National caddies to *Sports Illustrated*:

1. Willie "Pappy" Stokes
2. Nathaniel "Iron Man" Avery
3. Willie "Pete" Peterson
4. Carl "Skillet" Jackson
5. Eddie "E.B." McCoy
6. Ernest "Snipes" Nipper
7. Jerry "Bubba" Beard
8. Matthew "Shorty Mac" Palmer
9. Leon McCladdie
10. Mark "Banks" Eubanks

The Caddie Shack

Peak behind the bushes located to the right of the first fairway's landing area, just up from the gigantic Press Building. The area is off limits to tournament patrons, but it is where the soul of the Masters Tournament and Augusta National resides.

During tournament week, the smell of freshly grilled hamburgers, chicken strips, and French fries wafts through the tall pines. Walk around the parked semis that hauled in an assortment of goods, including the on-course concessions of pimento cheese sandwiches and ham sandwiches. The smell from the grill serves as a guidepost for the noses of approaching caddies, the police force, other security personnel, and various volunteers who know of the throwback to another day. Picnic tables sit to the side as another busy Masters round is in progress.

Appropriately, the cook's name is Herbert Fryer, himself a former caddie, who asks for orders in rapid-fire succession, occasionally missing the details of an order, but who cares when it tastes and smells this good. A window where the orders are taken is hidden behind the semis as a line of approximately one dozen people waits patiently. A makeshift sign hangs near the order window:

> Hamburgers and cheeseburgers, $1.50
> Chicken strips, $2
> Fries, 50 cents

Soda, 50 cents
         Diet Coke
         Root Beer
         Lemonade
         Orange

Hands down, the best meal on the grounds can be had here, with a good helping on a simple paper plate, eaten on an adjacent green picnic table. Compare the fare that is $6 cheaper than the same burger you can order in the more famous grill room at the clubhouse.

Step inside the caddie shack, just to the right of the grill window, and you will find a basic square room with green lockers against the walls, giving the appearance of the visiting locker room at a middle-sized college football stadium. The

The old caddie shack was located where the main spectator entrance to the grounds is now situated. The simple building was nothing more than a small room with lockers and at one time housed a pool table, a makeshift heater, a deep fryer and tables. A new, more modern facility with a full locker room, offices and kitchen was built in 1994. (© Augusta Chronicle)

facility was built in 1994. The caddie master, Tom Van Dorn, is holed up in an office just to the left of the main glassed entrance. Boxes of white Foot-Joy tennis shoes are stacked to the ceiling, awaiting the fittings like the shoe store at the local mall. Of course, just about everything is green or white.

This is where all caddies come to be fitted for the traditional white jumpsuit. Professional caddies, such as Stevie Williams, Tiger Woods' famous caddie, come by here daily to don the jumpsuit. Caddie novices also check in here, such as Jane Storm, the mother of English amateur Graeme Storm. She worked for her son in the 2000 Masters and needed quite a tailor's job to make the suit fit properly on her slight build. Friends and relatives of players, even the small children who work the Par-3 Contest, also drop by to deck out in the suit. Longtime Augusta National caddies still in the caddie corps hang out here just in case somebody needs an emergency caddie. This is also where the daily ritual of determining who gets a bag during regular member play is carried out. You will not find the Masters participants' golf bags here however; they are stored in an extension to the clubhouse that is located just to the right of the first tee.

This is a vast improvement over the former caddie shack, which was located where the main corridor of historical displays and a humongous outdoor golf shop are now packed with fans during Masters Week. That caddie shack was no more than a small room, which at one time had a pool table, a makeshift heater for cold days, a deep fryer for making all sorts of meals, and tables set up for all-day card games. It was where the Augusta National caddies hung out in their glory days.

One sense of history does prevail here in the new caddie shack. Pictures of the "Masters Caddie Hall of Fame" adorn the walls above the lockers inside the locker room, albeit just the caddies who have worked here since Caddie Master Enterprises took over in 1996. The framed pictures display the photos and accompanying nicknames of Bull, Hop, Skinny, Po Baby, Day Break, and many more.

Six of the regular crew who are still on staff have worked

here for more than fifty years, guys like Frank "Skinny" Ware; Johnny Garrett, better known as "Harrisburg", who first caddied here in 1940; and Johnny Frank Moore, who caddied for Gay Brewer's win in 1967. They form an encyclopedia of green-reading knowledge.

"Some of those guys were here when Ike's Tree was just a baby," says Joe Collins, himself a veteran caddie dating back to the 1960s. "They're living history."

The Jumpsuit

The most famous caddie garb in the world is also closely associated with painters and chicken and pig farmers.

Walk into International Uniform in the 1200 block of Broad Street in downtown Augusta—about five miles door to door from Augusta National—and you are in the middle of a typical mid-sized city's uniform store. Uniforms hang throughout the store for the medical and culinary fields and coveralls for all types of industrial and blue-collar jobs. However, in one corner, just to the left of the front door, is a hint that this is not the typical uniform supplier. There is the logo of Pinehurst Resort and Country Club in North Carolina on a caddie bib and, just down the wall, the bright white jumpsuit with the forest green lettering PALMER on the back.

This is the origination point of the famous caddie jumpsuits worn every day by Augusta National Golf Club caddies, made particularly famous during the Masters Tournament. The white long-sleeved jumpsuit, with the all-green Augusta National logo on the right breast pocket, the caddie number on the left breast pocket, and the player name Velcroed on the back, is made right here.

Any Ol' Joe can walk in this door, pluck down his twenty-seven dollars and walk out with what some think is a piece of history. The white "coveralls," as they are called in the industry, are specifically made for painters, chicken and pig farmers who need the white coloring to make sure infection does not spread from one area to another in their work, and for "clean-room" inspectors who also require a sterile environment.

"I sell blank coveralls all the time and some of the people that buy them I know aren't our typical customers. They probably put logos on it, sell it, whatever. But I can't control that. I would never do anything illegal or unethical," says Fred A. Daitch, the forty-four-year-old third-generation owner of International Uniforms.

The jumpsuit that Daitch makes for Augusta National is the vastly improved descendant of the suits initially worn at the Masters in 1946 when a handmade, hand-sewn herring-bone jumpsuit debuted for the first Masters after World War II. In the first eight Masters, caddies usually dressed similar to the gallery, with a coat and tie, some type of fedora or pancake

One of the earliest known photos of caddies at the Augusta National Golf Club, taken some time in the early 1930s. Notice the caddies' dress, before the utilization of the famed jumpsuits that the Augusta National caddies have worn for more than fifty years. (© Historic Golf Photos/Ron Watts Collection)

hat stylish in that day, and for a few of these years a simple cut-out number pinned on their back to identify the players. Many also dressed like a farmer's hand, with denim coveralls, or in woolen jackets and casual clothing, something akin to what Jed Clampett wore in the 1960s television comedy *The Beverly Hillbillies.* The dress was not standardized as even the hats differed; witness the tall, silk hat that Gene Sarazen's caddie, Stovepipe, wore in the 1935 Masters. Therefore, with Augusta National having a penchant for uniformity, the uniform was born.

Daitch's grandfather, Philip, formed Daitch and Company in 1930 to provide industrial uniforms to the public. Along the way, probably some time in the 1940s, he and his son, Irvin, started providing Augusta National with various items for the tournament, particularly vinyl raincoats, and, eventually, the simple white coveralls with no logos. At first, Augusta National caddies wore the prescribed uniform of green denim coveralls topped by a green cap with a yellow button during regular member play and then evidently wore the more sporty white uniform during Masters play before the white suit became the calling card in the 1950s.

In its April 12, 1950, edition, *Golf World* reported "the Negro caddies were clad in white coveralls and green baseball caps, plainly numbered in green across their backs."

Irvin and sons Gary and Fred would fill a U-Haul with raincoats, truck them out to the tournament, and if the seal on the trailer was broken, Augusta National would have to buy raincoats.

"We, of course, prayed for rain at the Masters," jokes Fred.

Fred, who changed the name to International Uniform after his father passed away in 1995, is not a golf junkie even though he was born and raised in Augusta. He has attended the Masters for years and once made a brief visit to the Richmond County Jail for attempting to scalp a Masters Series Badge as a college student in the early 1980s. He does cherish the 1960s hand-made caddie jumpsuit that is on display in Neil Ghingold Antiques two doors down from his store. Fred has made informal overtures with Neil to purchase it, simply because it may have been one of the first caddie jumpsuits his family provided to Augusta National. But, Fred just took up golf within the last year. He most often rents his home during Masters Week and takes the family on vacation. Moreover, he does not know most of the world's most famous golfers by name.

But he does know a good business deal when he sees one.

That is the reason he cherishes the Augusta National business connection. In 1996, when Caddie Master Enterprises began supervising the caddies at Augusta National, Fred did not get a caddie jumpsuit order from Augusta National early that year. Curious why, he called the club and was told it had changed plans for the supplier of its caddie jumpsuits. Fred quickly inquired the price with new Augusta National caddie master Tom Van Dorn and was told twenty-seven dollars per order. He replied that he could provide the same product for nineteen dollars, and produce it locally, including other area vendors in the process. He kept the Augusta National account and gained a slew of Caddie Master Enterprises clients as the word spread about his business.

"The reason I price like I do is I want to own the market," Daitch says. "My goal really and truly is to own the golf market as far as caddie wear is concerned."

Within the last few years, his caddie wear business has "truly been a snowball rolling slowly downhill," Daitch says. After attending the PGA Merchandise Show in Orlando in 2001 and 2002, his line of caddie jumpsuits, bibs, sand bags, and belts grew from ten percent of his business to twenty-five percent as of autumn 2002. His biggest concern at the first Merchandise Show in 2001 was not getting enough business, but how his small operation could handle an ordering feast where he wrote $10,000 worth of business in the first two hours of the show. He was able to phone home to his wife after the first day of the show and tell her to go ahead and purchase a new car, with cash.

The thing that caught everyone's eye at the Merchandise Show in Daitch's simple 10 by 10 foot booth was the mannequin display with the Masters caddie jumpsuit. Golf pros stood

This old caddie uniform is displayed on a mannequin at Neil Ghingold Antiques on Broad Street in downtown Augusta. Ghingold believes the jumpsuit was worn by Claude Harmon's caddie. The number 105 would indicate that Harmon's caddie wore the jump suit in 1962 when the Masters had its largest field ever, 109 players. That is the only Masters where the field exceeded 103 players. (Photograph by Michael Holahan, © *Augusta Chronicle*)

two and three deep to get a glance at this new vendor. One of those onlookers drawn in by the crowd was Dave Spencer, the longtime co-head professional at Augusta National. Concerned that the Augusta National name was being commercialized, Spencer requested that the logo be taken off the jumpsuit, and Daitch quickly complied. Ten minutes later, Spencer returned.

"The white coverall is symbolic of Augusta National and the Masters," Daitch recalls Spencer saying. "I'd appreciate it if you would take the whole white coverall out of the booth."

Daitch removed the white jumpsuit, with quick apologies to Spencer. Clubs such as Pinehurst Resort and Dallas National had emphatically requested that their emblems be displayed in the booth. They wanted their name affiliated with the product.

But the show had proven that Daitch's calling card was the Augusta National–branded jumpsuits. By 2003, one of Augusta National's most popular items was the sale of commemorative Beanie Babies in its on-site stores. That was nothing new since the club had previously sold the small items, first as pure green bears. But this time the small bears were dressed in a caddie jumpsuit, with the No. 1 on the front breast pocket, a MASTERS name tag on the back, and the green baseball cap on the head. Customers rushed to buy the product as word spread among collectors.

Daitch has even endured a couple incidents when Augusta National officials called to complain about the slightest flaw in his work.

In 1998, Daitch was laid up in an Augusta hospital, suffering from a recurring gastrointestinal disorder, probably stirred up by stress, which resulted in internal bleeding. He had already rented his home for the week and was planning another family vacation. It was the evening of the first Masters practice round and Daitch's cellular phone rang in his hospital room. With IVs in his arm and woozy from medication, he answered to the sound of an angry Augusta National employee berating him because the green lettering of approximately ten player names from the back of the jumpsuits had bled onto the rest of the garment when they were washed. They needed replacement name tags, immediately. Daitch never mentioned he was in the hospital or that this was normally a two-week process. He called his secretary at home, coaxed the printer out of a son's Little League baseball game and into working overnight, and then he promptly fell asleep, exhausted. When he woke up the next day at approximately noon, Daitch nervously called his secretary and heard the great news that the new names had been hand-delivered to the caddie shack that Tuesday at 7 A.M., just in time for the first players out for a second day of practice.

"I've been to hell and back for them," Daitch says. "But that is what has made us the best in the industry. We have to come up to the standards of Augusta National. Our name tags

Fred Daitch, the owner of International Uniform on Broad Street in downtown Augusta, displays a caddie bib *(left)* that he provides for Pinehurst (N.C.) Resort and Country Club and the patented jumpsuit that the Augusta National Golf Club and the Masters Tournament use for their caddies. Daitch's father started the business and may have been the first to provide the jumpsuits for caddies at Augusta National. (Photograph by Michael Holahan, © *Augusta Chronicle*)

have to be level and can't be one-quarter of an inch off. Augusta National would notice and send them right back. Being forced to come up to their standards makes anything we do acceptable to anybody else. I have never had a complaint from another caddie-wear customer. These clubs rant and rave about what we do. If Augusta National put these challenges in front of most companies, they would probably think some of their requests were ridiculous, too picky. It's been a blessing in disguise."

Daitch provides the basic, no-frills jumpsuit for regular play at Augusta National and the more famous version for the tournament, complete with all the logos and an ever-improving system of using Velcro to stick the player's name on the back of the uniform. In the early years of the jumpsuit's use through the 1980s, the name and Masters logo were stitched on and prone to break loose and flap in the breeze. Augusta National receives sizes X-Small to XXX-Large to better fit the gamut of caddies from English amateur Graeme Storm's tiny mother in 2000 to seven-feet-one San Antonio Spurs center David Robinson, who caddied for friend Corey Pavin in the Par-3 Contest in the mid-1990s. Augusta National might have to do some on-site tailoring, but at least the sizes are close.

The complaint by many caddies is that the jumpsuits are hot or, simply, too bothersome. They differ from the standard wear of a professional caddie today—sneakers, shorts, and golf shirt covered with a simple sleeveless bib that bears the tournament sponsor's name and comes with a pocket in the front for placement of pencils, scorecard, and yardage book. The Memorial Tournament, Jack Nicklaus' PGA Tour event in Dublin, Ohio, is the rare exception to that dress. Caddies at Jack's event wear a similar jumpsuit—giving a nod to the Golden Bear's affection for the Masters—but with a lighter-weight material and short sleeves.

Augusta National's caddies are also instructed to wear the Foot-Joy brand shoes, white with a touch of green outline, instead of their normal athletic shoes. Outside caddies have the option to wear their customary footwear but are asked to use white shoes. Still, shoe boxes are stacked ceiling high in the caddie shack, awaiting the odd foot sizes from the very small for children of players to the very large to fit the large feet of caddies such as Carl Jackson or Robinson. Once, years ago, the caddies even wore the canvas, high-top Converse basketball shoes, more famously called "Chucks" for inventor Chuck Taylor.

Until 1999, caddies on the PGA Tour were required to wear long pants during tournaments. After lobbying for a softening of the policy, shorts were allowed on the Tour if the heat index reached 100 degrees. That was broadened even further to allow for shorts in any event, but with the stipulation that they be Tour-dispersed navy or blue with the Tour logo on the bottom. That too was eventually altered to today's standard, allowing any color but no cutoffs, cargo shorts, or gym shorts.

Many caddies wear bare bones under the Augusta National jumpsuit, usually a pair of gym or standard shorts and a T-shirt or golf shirt. Some have taken a dare and worn nothing but underwear—or even less—under the jumpsuit to get better "ventilation." When the weather gets cold, the jumpsuit is welcomed as another layer to hold off the elements. But when Augusta gets hot and humid ...

"Quite a few guys wore nothing under them," says Donnie Wanstall, a former Tour caddie who worked for Mark O'Meara for years and toted for Japan's Tommy Nakajima in the 1983 Masters. "If it was cold I might have worn a long-sleeve T-shirt and some jeans under them. But when it was hot, it was nothing. When I got through for the day, I just got dressed in the caddie facility privately and then put the suit in the dirty laundry. I wasn't telling anybody that I wasn't wearing anything underneath."

That is exactly the reason that Jariah Beard always wore his normal clothes underneath. The former Augusta National caddie said, "I wanted to be sure that everything was clean. Who knows who wore it before I did?"

Daitch says that the jumpsuits' 65 percent polyester–35 percent cotton makeup is more heat resistant than 100 percent cotton or even the shorts, golf shirts, and bibs that caddies wear most of the year. He also says that the caddies should not wear clothes underneath the jumpsuits, which the majority do, but just underwear and, at most, an accompanying T-shirt. He says the polyester component does not wrinkle easily, a very important factor to Augusta National officials.

Daitch's association with the caddie jumpsuits has spread simply by word of mouth. Scott Verplank, a veteran PGA Tour member, called to get his son Scottie a custom-fitted version in time for a caddying job in the Par-3 Contest a few years back. Daitch did not set a fee for that request. He just asked that Scott send golf memorabilia for various charitable auctions, which he did. Some players who get their young children to join in the casual atmosphere of the Par-3 Contest on Wednesday have followed suit.

A new client club in Jamaica called recently to order jumpsuits, and Daitch suggested they get short sleeves because of the hot weather in the Caribbean, but the club insisted on the Augusta National–style long-sleeve version.

Funny how far a simple white outfit can go.

Picking the Numbers
of a Masters Champion

The unlucky numbers for the Augusta National caddies are 1 and 13. Sometimes.

Every caddie is assigned a number to assist the fans in determining the names of players, using that day's Masters pairing sheet as a reference. The numbering system began before the caddie jumpsuits were first used in 1946. The first recorded numbering of caddies, according to Augusta National Golf Club documentation, was in 1941 when winner Craig Wood's caddie wore No. 30, even though Sam Snead posed for a photograph with a caddie wearing a number on his back in the late 1930s. In those early days, players' names were not worn, only a number. The only identifying element was a makeshift piece of paper with a number, taped to the back of the caddie's jacket or shirt.

The only player who receives a designated number is the defending champion. The No. 1 is always reserved for him. The remainder of the numbers given to caddies and their players are determined by the order in which the players check in at registration during tournament week, which begins the Saturday before. Fans can usually assess which players have put in the most practice time at the course during tournament week by checking out the single digits and teens on their pairing sheets.

Veteran players such as Jack Nicklaus or Tiger Woods usually wear high numbers, unless they draw the defending champion's No. 1, because they limit their tournament week on-site preparation. Nicklaus used to be famous for coming to Augusta the week before the Masters to get in his practice time uninterrupted, usually playing regularly with member Billy Morris, and then returned a couple days before the tournament competition began. Woods will usually drop by a couple weeks before the tournament to quickly determine the course characteristics that year, and then work out in Augusta National–like conditions at his home course, Isleworth Country Club, in Orlando, Florida.

Ben Hogan combined those two strategies. He prepared at Seminole Golf Club, his home course in south Florida, in the weeks leading up to the tournament, playing matches against the likes of Claude Harmon, the head pro and 1948 Masters champion. Hogan would travel to Augusta as soon as the week before the tournament to hit balls in the practice area and develop a game plan. When Hogan won in 1951 and 1953, caddie "Pappy" Stokes wore No. 6 and No. 2, respectively.

The numbering system even inspired a nickname. John Henry Williams, the caddie master from just after World War II until his death in 1959, was simply called "Eleven" because that was the number he wore as a caddie before becoming caddie master.

It should come as no surprise that No. 13 was the first number to concern the Masters participant.

In 1938, Snead's caddie O'Bryant Williams was given the No. 13. The jovial Snead posed for a front-page *Augusta Chronicle* photograph as he pinned the unlucky number on his caddie, who was dressed in dark trousers, jacket, and hat as if he had just walked out of a church service. Snead joked that the number, which resembled the size and material that track-and-field athletes wear, would result in "the worst nine I've ever played since joining the professional ranks."

Snead shot a 2-under 34 on the front nine in the first round, but then played poorly on the back nine to shoot 44 for what would be his worst nine holes in tournament history.

Arnold Palmer turned No. 13 into his own lucky number. After Palmer's caddie "Iron Man" Avery wore No. 85 in the duo's first Masters victory in 1958, Palmer was given No. 13 for 1960. He birdied the last two holes to win the tournament. Two years later, in 1962, "Iron Man" again sported No. 13 for a second Palmer win. Arnie had No. 82 in his last Masters victory in 1964.

Jack Nicklaus *(right)* and caddie Willie Peterson on the way to Jack's second consecutive Masters title in 1966. Nicklaus became the first Masters champion to defend the title. Notice Peterson's No. 90 uniform. Nicklaus refused to take the No. 1 reserved for the defending champion, using his superstitions to pick No. 90, the number he wore in capturing the 1965 title. (© *Augusta Chronicle*)

The number 13 is one of fourteen numbers that caddies have worn to multiple Masters titles. The numbers 6 and 52 have each been worn a record three times each by the victor. Hogan (1951), Gay Brewer (1967), and Seve Ballesteros (1983) all wore No. 6. Gary Player won in 1961 and 1978 and Ben Crenshaw in 1984 with No. 52.

No. 1 has been quite superstitious also.

When Nicklaus returned to Augusta in 1966 to defend his 1965 Masters title, the Golden Bear refused to take No. 1, the defending champion's number. Nicklaus was aiming to become the first man to repeat. He opted instead for No. 90, the number caddie Willie Peterson wore in 1965.

"A No. 1 has never won this tournament, you know," Nicklaus said the week before the 1966 Masters as he went through his usual pre-Masters Week practice routine. "The fact of no repeaters doesn't bother me, really it doesn't make one bit of difference. I would just like things to be like last year."

Nicklaus jokingly said the plan was to take the superstitious attitude beyond the golf course.

"I'm going home (to Palm Beach, Florida) Saturday. I'm going to try and leave at precisely the same moment that I did last year. I've even told the lady we rented the house from to put the same dirty sheets back on the bed."

Nicklaus' caddie did not always wear No. 90. Peterson wore No. 49 in 1963, No. 16 in 1972, and No. 76 in 1975. Jack Nicklaus II wore No. 89 for his father's sixth Masters title in 1986.

Nicklaus' 90 is the highest number a caddie has ever worn to win the Masters. On three occasions, in 1957 (101), 1962 (109), and 1966 (103), the field pushed into triple digits, bringing on the huge numbers on the back of the jumpsuits.

The two back-to-back champions since have broken the No. 1 curse. Nick Faldo's caddie Fanny Sunesson took No. 1 when Faldo repeated in 1990, although Andy Prodger was Faldo's caddie in 1989. Tiger Woods' caddie Steve Williams wore No. 1 in 2002 after displaying No. 71 in 2001.

If No. 1 was originally unlucky, then No. 32 was very lucky for Tom Watson. Leon McCladdie took Watson's bag in 1977 and wore No. 32. Watson won his first Masters that year. When Watson won the 1981 tournament, McCladdie once again wore No. 32.

"Any number you win with is lucky," McCladdie said in 1981. "This is the first time since (Watson) won in 1977 that we've had it again. I knew we would win."

The End of an Era, 1982–1983

It was Friday, April 9, 1982, a cool, damp morning, when the exclusivity of Augusta National caddies in the Masters came crashing down. Weather was a factor, but inattention to detail was the biggest fault.

Thursday's first round has been among the most difficult days in tournament history. Rain halted play at 4:30 P.M. with thirty-six players still on the course. A continuous drizzle hit the players all day and the temperature never reached more than 48 degrees. The new bent grass greens, being used for the second time in Masters competition, were even faster than normal because of the cool weather. Conditions were so difficult that Fuzzy Zoeller's even-par 72 led the field of those who completed first-round play. Frank Conner shot 89 and Jim Thorpe 88. Herman Keiser, the 1946 Masters champion making his farewell appearance, withdrew after a 93.

"Hell no, let 'em play, I think they'll enjoy it," Zoeller cracked about calling off play after completing his first round.

"It'll be cold (on Friday)," two-time champion Tom Watson said. "The lakes will be frozen. We won't have to worry about carrying those holes. We'll be able to drive No. 10 (where there was casual water on Friday) and No. 11. We won't have to worry about Rae's Creek on 12 and 13."

As the rain-delayed first round resumed at 7:30 A.M. on Friday, many players were literally left holding their bags, scurrying for last-second caddies. David Graham's wife was forced into duty on the driving range, shagging balls as her husband prepared to complete his first round. Some players' clubs were even still wet from the day before. Some Augusta National caddies had presumed that the first round was washed out, with players retaining their same tee times for Friday. LeRoy Schultz said his boss Tom Weiskopf even told him that his tee time for Friday would be the same as for the first round. Some caddies stayed out late Thursday night partying and were still asleep when play began and others simply arrived late, unaware of the early start.

Still, the *Augusta Chronicle* story on Friday morning clearly stated, "The 36 left on the course will tee off at 7:30 A.M. today. At completion of the first round, new three-man pairings will be made and second-round play will begin around 11:30 A.M. from both the No. 1 and No 10 tees."

"The problem was that they didn't show up," Watson said in 1983. "What do you do? Carry your own bag? Use pull carts? Some of us had to take whoever was available as caddies."

At tournament's end, Watson was most notable among the players who wrote Augusta National chairman Hord W. Hardin about instituting a change. Watson, the 1977 and 1981 champion with Leon McCladdie on the bag, also spoke with Hardin about the request.

"Suppose you had to go into your biggest trial and you were told you couldn't use your own legal secretary? That's what it's like for us at Augusta," Watson told Hardin, a retired attorney.

"Mr. Watson, you plead a very strong case," Hardin responded.

The movement by Tour players to bring their own caddies to the tournament had been building for years. Until 1962, the United States Golf Association considered a caddie, caddie master, or anyone who worked at a golf club cleaning or repairing clubs to be a professional. Until 1974, all four major championships banned the use of outside caddies. By 1975, the PGA Championship at Firestone Country Club in Akron, Ohio, and the British Open at Carnoustie, Scotland, had opened their doors to outside caddies. The U.S. Open followed suit one year later. Ironically, the U.S. Open first allowed caddies that were not attached to the host club for the 1976 tournament at the Atlanta Athletic Club, Bobby Jones' home course in Atlanta. Of the 150 players in the field at that U.S. Open, 104 brought their own caddies. For the 1976 British Open, Nicklaus' longtime caddie for the overseas event, Jimmy Dickinson, pulled up lame in a practice round and Jack's oldest son, fifteen-year-old Jack II, stepped in to tote for his dad, ten years before the miracle Masters of 1986. Jackie even played the role of the lucky caddie on the morning of the final round by—unbeknownst to Jack and Barbara Nicklaus—donning the clothes he had worn weeks earlier in capturing a junior golf tournament in Columbus, Ohio.

Only the Masters and Western Open remained off limits to Tour caddies by 1982. The Masters held fast simply because of its tradition of providing caddies. The Western remained true because of its longstanding charitable effort via the Chick Evans Scholarship Foundation, a program of providing college scholarships for caddies that began in 1930 and prominently continues today. Chicago-area caddies alone worked at the Western Open until 1986, but by 1987, Tour caddies were allowed.

"My caddie had been with me through all the good finishes I had there, so I can't say he's a bad caddie, but he showed up late twice last year," Tom Kite said at Augusta in 1983. "My Tour caddie has worked for me four and a half years and he's never been late."

"The caddies at Augusta have gotten progressively worse," said Raymond Floyd, the 1976 champion. "Most of them take a week off from their regular job to caddie. They're not caddies and they don't know yardages. The caddie I won with (Hop Harrison) is a mill worker who's been taking the week off to work at the National.

"I can accept going into one or two tournaments a year (not using his own caddie), but last year when most of them didn't show up to complete play ... that killed them. A lot of players had been very vocal about it for a long time. The seed was planted. When they didn't show up last year, that did it."

"There's no question the Augusta National caddies aren't as conscientious as they used to be," said four-time Masters champion Arnold Palmer.

Even Lee Elder, who made his historic debut as the first black to play in a Masters in 1975, had gripes about the caddies. He was welcomed enthusiastically by the entire caddie corps when he came to play practice rounds and during tournament week. Henry Brown, a thirty-six-year-old Augusta cab driver, was given the job, much to Elder's pleasure ... at first. Brown, who professed to have worked at Augusta National since 1952, was a cross-handed golfer who sported a 1 handicap and was invited to play in an Elder Pro-Am event in Virginia in May 1975. Brown had also caddied for Roberto De Vicenzo when the Argentine golfer incorrectly signed his scorecard in 1968, thereby losing by one stroke to Bob Goalby. But Elder later revealed that the caddie did not show that much skill carrying the bag.

"My caddie would tell me which club to use for approaches instead of telling me the yardage and letting me make my own club selections," Elder told the *Washington Post* in 1976. "I'd be fifteen or twenty feet beyond the pin. I could have eliminated the problem by firing him and getting someone else after the first round (he opted not to) ... I'm not trying to use him as an excuse, but it happens to be the truth."

PGA Tour caddies were grumbling behind the scenes at the 1982 event that they were considering a class-action discrimination suit against Augusta National or the sponsors of the tournament. They argued that you had to be black to caddie in the Masters and they were being denied the right to work.

One undisclosed Tour caddie was in attendance at the 1982 Masters and voiced his displeasure over the Augusta National caddie's performance to *Golf World*.

My player would hand his ball (for the caddie to clean) after marking on the green, and there wasn't anyone there. He was told not to help my man read greens but tried anyway and didn't know from beans. He got real active when we got to the televised holes. One day my man had to awaken his caddie, who was fast asleep on the bag at the putting green ... I talked to Augusta caddies and they said they had to caddie at the club at least two weeks in one year's time to be eligible for drawing assignments in the Masters. Two weeks won't teach you a thing. Then I asked if I could put in two weeks, and the unison reply was, "Man, you are the wrong color." If this is true then that sure as heck is discrimination and restraint of trade.

As Augusta National opened for membership play in October 1982, one of Hardin's first orders of business was to finalize a new caddie policy. Some members disagreed with allowing outside caddies; they wanted to be true to their home caddies. Hardin called the decision-making process "traumatic," with the players' wishes winning out.

On November 10, 1982, the closing bell rang on the exclusive use of Augusta National caddies in the Masters. Hardin made the following statement about why the caddie force was opened.

The advent of the golf cart has made caddies a dying breed. Many clubs have none at all. That fact, coupled with the enormous growth of the professional circuit in this country and elsewhere, has created a new phenomenon—the Tour caddie.

The latter normally works for the same professional wherever he plays, frequently is an accomplished player in his own right, knows his man's swing characteristics and has been known to provide helpful advice in that area during play. He knows his man's preferences as to caddie procedures and is careful to comply herewith. Perhaps more importantly, he works week after week under highly competitive tournament conditions. In fact, he and the player are a team—a partnership.

Despite the general excellence of our Augusta caddies, the players are absolutely convinced that their own performances will be better if they can use their regular caddies. We have concluded therefore that it is very important to the player competing for one of golf's four major titles that he be comfortable with his caddie.

Before the 1983 tournament, Hardin addressed the issue further.

"We're not naive enough to say we have eighty caddies who can be classified at the same level as Tour caddies," he said. "If I were a player under today's conditions, and I think Bobby Jones would agree, I would want to bring my own caddie."

That decision may have been the reason many of the long-time Augusta National caddies despised Hardin and cherished the old realm of Clifford Roberts. They said that Hardin did not show them due respect in the transition. Roberts was noted for creating a charitable foundation at Augusta National and using funds from it to support former caddies who were having a difficult time. He also encouraged guests to pay the caddie "what you think he's worth" during a round, usually urging them to pay more than the standard fee.

"Our members are gonna take care of us," Hop Harrison said in 1983. "I've called one member before who lives 300 miles away, needing money, and he has sent me $300 or $400. They're gonna take good care of us. They'll take better care of us than our chairman."

Nevertheless, the deed had been done and the 1983 Masters had a new feel to it. There was some friction in the caddie shack, usually an uncomfortable silence when outside caddies came in to get their jumpsuits. Willie Peterson, Jack Nicklaus' caddie, had a confrontation with Jack Tosone, amateur Jim Hallett's caddie, when Tosone was the first caddie to register for the tournament and got locker No. 1, a position Willie believed he deserved.

Augusta National changed many things for the new caddie corps.

Yardage books were available for the first time to accommodate the outside caddies who were not quite as familiar with Augusta National. Previously, the Augusta National caddies went by their trained eye. They had used rudimentary yardage guides that were prepared by the superintendent or checked a diagram of the hole location for that day that had been placed on each tee box. "Gorgeous" George Lucas, a former PGA Tour caddie and experienced course surveyor, was hired by the club to visit Augusta National and precisely measure the course to devise his creative, hand-drawn, wallet-sized yardage guide.

Lucas is a former caddie for many players, including Arnold Palmer, from the early 1970s until the early 1980s. He earned his nickname in the 1970s when Lanny Wadkins' caddie, with whom he was a roommate on the road, noticed the large supply of toiletry items that George was carrying in his suitcase and dubbed him "Gorgeous" after the famous professional wrestler. Lucas' calling of creating yardage books began in 1976 and was starting to become a trademark on the PGA Tour—and continues today—as caddies were provided with more and more guidance as they prepared their players.

Lucas met with Hardin and other club staff members in the chairman's crowded office to review the process. Lucas used a wire cable to precisely measure the golf course. (He uses a laser gun and reflective prisms today for the more than 1,000 courses he has measured in over twenty-five years on the job.) He did not charge for his initial services on the prestigious grounds "because it would have been like charging to go to church." Instead, he was offered a tournament badge and a parking pass for the players' lot during that year's tournament.

Lucas' books give exact distances from various spots on the holes, utilizing the usual places such as sprinkler heads and trees and the unusual landmarks such as abrupt changes in elevation to enable caddies to calculate distances. He also denoted the depth and rolls in the greens and added the subtle, humorous references such as "J.I.C." (Just In Case) for odd positions on the course, "Grand Daddy Choco-Drop" for mounding in the fifteenth fairway, and "H2O" with a fish figure for water hazards.

One of the first books, with the standard green cover including the Masters logo and YARDAGE in block letters, gave attribution to Lucas inside the front cover as follows: "The distances contained in this book were compiled and measured by George L. Lucas II. Although the information is believed to be correct, the Augusta National Golf Club does not guarantee its accuracy."

George Lucas was hired in 1983 to produce new yardage books for the caddie corps at the Masters Tournament in preparation for the influx of outside caddies at that year's tournament. The pocket-sized book, as shown from a mid-1980s version, had a simple green cover with the Masters logo and a brief description of the symbols used in Lucas' drawings. Notice the Augusta National disclaimer for Lucas' measurements. (Reprinted with the permission of George Lucas)

The distances contained in this book were compiled and measured by George L. Lucas, II. Although this information is believed to be correct, the Augusta National Golf Club does not guarantee its accuracy.

COMPILED &
MEASURED BY:
GEORGE L. LUCAS, II

ABBREVIATIONS

1. ⊕ SPRINKLER HEAD

2. ALL MEASUREMENTS TO FRONT EDGE OF GREEN, UNLESS OTHERWISE STATED.

3. F.L. -- FRONT LEFT EDGE GREEN
    F.R. -- FRONT RIGHT
    B.L. -- BACK LEFT
    B.R. -- BACK RIGHT

4. DEPTH OF GREEN GIVEN AT TOP OF GREEN (AT BACK EDGE).

5. ⊤ -- INDICATES DISTANCE TO BACK CUT OF CHAMPIONSHIP TEES.

6. ⊥ -- INDICATES DISTANCE TO FRONT CUT OF GREEN.

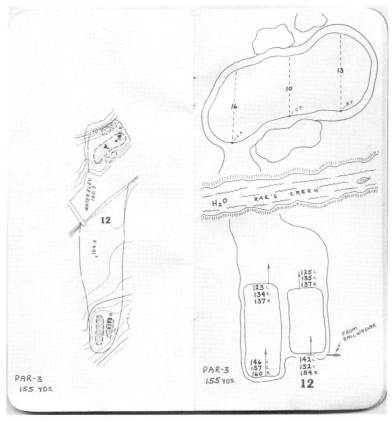

This sketch of the famous par-3 twelfth hole gives the various yardages from the tee boxes and the depth of the green. Notice the fish symbol drawn on the right side of Rae's Creek. (Reprinted with the permission of George Lucas)

Most players acclaimed the new books. Even Nicklaus, who had charted the course during his twenty-plus years playing in the Masters, started to use the new information.

Range balls were also available for the first time, with six different brands offered so that players could warm up with their accustomed specifications. Previously, players wanted the true feel of their own equipment so they brought a shag bag. Old, out-of-round golf balls that were provided by public ranges did not satisfy the players and most clubs that hosted tournaments did not even consider practice balls to be necessary.

The dangerous practice of shagging balls on the range was also banned. Even though the routine offered an extra caddie fee, it was tortuous. Imagine having no catcher's gear and only a towel to fend off a golf ball traveling like a bullet from over 150 yards away. The custom of caddies standing in the landing area of a practice range as players hit their own balls in their general direction was commonplace until the late 1970s in the United States and into the 1980s on the European Tour. When dozens of players were practicing at the same time, it was almost comical to see caddies dodging balls hit by other players as they eyed their own man. Before the creation of the current short-game practice facility on the south side of Magnolia Lane, both sides of the famous entryway to the clubhouse were utilized for practice with all clubs.

Caddies would step back toward the far end of the range as their players progressed through the bag toward their drivers. Many used towels or even an occasional baseball mitt to flag down balls on the fly—therefore the baseball term *shagging*—while others took the safer route of one-hopping balls. Some players practiced diagonally so that their caddies could be situated on the edge of the practice area, thereby eliminating some of the friendly fire. Others simply found a schoolyard or park for warm-ups instead of subjecting their caddies to bombardment. Legend has it that Hogan's caddies adjusted their towels from one hand to the other only when Hogan was practicing a draw or a fade. But many a caddie developed battle scars from being drilled in the stomach, shoulders, or even around the head, especially on cloudy days when the white golf ball was difficult to follow against the backdrop of clouds.

In all, eighteen Augusta National caddies had jobs in the eighty-one-player field for 1983. That included Peterson with Nicklaus, Carl Jackson with Ben Crenshaw, Matthew Palmer with Billy Casper, Eddie McCoy with Gary Player, LeRoy Schultz with Weiskopf, and Ben Bussey with defending champion Craig Stadler. Leon McCladdie, Watson's caddie in his two Masters victories in 1977 and 1981, even got a bag, with amateur Robert Lewis Jr.

"Since I won with him, I thought he deserved another shot," Stadler said of Bussey.

One of the surprise changes was Fuzzy Zoeller going with his regular Tour caddie Mike Mazzeo. Fuzzy had planned on retaining his Augusta National caddie Jariah Beard but relented on the Friday before the tournament. Seve Ballesteros, who won in 1980 with Marion Herrington on his bag, won in 1983 with his regular Tour caddie Nicholas DePaul.

"Some guys, my best friends, say it doesn't feel like the Masters anymore," Jackson said in 1984.

Jackson also more recently said that the changeover could have had a positive effect on Crenshaw's first Masters victory in 1984. Crenshaw finished at 11-under par 277, two in front of Watson. The 1984 and 1995 wins by Crenshaw are the only wins by a caddie with Augusta National ties since 1982.

"I think it could have cost Tom Watson the '84 Masters," Jackson said. "He had a good caddie, Bruce Edwards. But Leon McCladdie was a great caddie, too, and really knew this course. We played with Tom on Saturday (in 1984) and because they didn't know a few things, that local knowledge, it helped us a few shots."

A handful of veteran caddies say that the Augusta National caddies would still be in service if Roberts were still around. However, it was inevitable that the ever-changing makeup of caddies would eventually come to the Masters. Many Masters veterans still say it would be beneficial for young players and first-time Masters participants to hire an Augusta National caddie to fully digest the subtle breaks of the greens and where to best hit approach shots.

"It really hurt when they did that to us," Beard said. "We lost a lot of pride. I know this would have eventually happened. But the way it was done was disrespectful. It could have been handled a whole lot better. That's all we asked.

"I had no problem with the outside caddies coming on. But make them earn their way like we did. Make them learn the course first, learn the greens. Some players even came in and brought their mommas, their daddies, their brothers to caddie for them. All we wanted was an equal chance."

First Female Caddie: Daughters, Sisters, Mothers, and Friends

The first female caddie in the Masters Tournament is now a Presbyterian minister.

Elizabeth Archer was a nineteen-year-old student at Stanford University majoring in American studies and international relations when she became the first female caddie in tournament history in 1983. It was the first year that non–Augusta National caddies were allowed in the tournament.

"I hadn't planned to do this," George Archer said in 1983. "But when mother and daughter go to work on you, you know who is going to win."

Elizabeth started caddying for her father, George, the 1969 Masters champion, in 1980 on a suggestion from her mother, Donna. It was a way to get closer to her father, who traveled quite often on the PGA Tour. She had the athletic ability to tote a heavy golf bag around the hilly Augusta National course, as she stood five-feet-eleven and threw the javelin and discus for Stanford's track and field team. To better prepare for those sports, she had begun a weight-lifting program in college.

Their first time together, in the 1980 Canadian Open at Royal Montreal Golf Club, George set his watch incorrectly for the earlier time zone, gave it to Elizabeth, and then George was late for his tee time the next morning. He was assessed a two-stroke penalty.

Elizabeth Archer, a Stanford University student at the time, became the first female caddie in Masters history when she worked for her father, 1969 Masters champion George Archer, during the 1983 Masters. (© *Augusta Chronicle*)

"Before I became his caddie, my father and I were never really close," Elizabeth said. "Then I got to see him do what he does best, and we started a friendship that first summer. How many kids get to know what their fathers do for a living? That's the neatest thing about it."

Even with two summers under her belt caddying on the PGA Tour, George was concerned about putting Elizabeth on his bag for the first Masters that allowed outside caddies.

"My first thought is it would be rocking the boat," Archer said in 1983, "especially since it is the first year that golfers have brought their own caddies."

Archer recorded a tie for twelfth finish in 1983. Two years later, younger daughter Marilyn became the second Archer girl and second female to work in the Masters.

Today, Elizabeth is a Presbyterian minister with a doctorate in theology.

Women caddying in the Masters has been a rarity, usually reserved for kin such as the Archer girls. Daughters, wives, sisters, and mothers have all worn the famous jumpsuits.

Nicole Stricker caddied for her husband Steve and Sheryl Calcavecchia for husband Mark. Both had caddied off and on for their husbands on the PGA Tour.

Shelley Green drew the spotlight in the 1986 Masters when she caddied for younger brother Ken in his Masters debut. Ken shared the first-round lead with Bill Kratzert and became a big story because of his offbeat personality (such as throwing his putter to his caddie, sneaking friends into the tournament in the trunk of his car, and wearing lime-green shoes) and the partnership with his twenty-nine-year-old sister. Shelley had left a bookkeeper's job in Connecticut a couple years before the 1986 Masters to move to Florida and be closer to her brother and warm weather. He gave Shelley, his full-time caddie that year, some credit, in an odd sort of way for the quick Masters start. He would eventually fade during the week, which was highlighted by Nick Price's course-record 63 in the third round and Jack Nicklaus' comeback on Sunday to win his sixth green jacket.

"She has no clue out there," Green said of his sister. "If she suggests something, I always do the opposite.

"She wasn't interested in learning about golf. That's the way it should be. I don't want a caddie that can make me second-guess myself. Too many caddies control the players sometimes, and I don't think that's right. I've seen too many caddies alter a player's decision."

Jane Storm is the only mother of a player who has ever caddied in a Masters, working with son Graeme, the British Amateur champion, in the 2000 Masters. Jane's small stature forced the Augusta National staff to make some alterations on the scene. They had to cut six inches off the arms and pants legs of her caddie jumpsuit so that she could have a snug fit. In the process, Jane tried on three different suits.

Graeme resisted hiring an Augusta National caddie because his mother had always been there for him.

"It just happened really," Graeme said. "She would drive me to the golf tournaments as a young player (in England) and then stay around and caddie for me. She was going to have to be there to take me home anyway."

Fanny Sunesson has been the most successful female caddie and one of the winningest caddies in Masters history. The Swede was on Nick Faldo's bag during two of his three victories, in 1990 and 1996.

"I don't like doing anything. I don't like being in the press," Sunesson said after Faldo won the 1990 Masters.

Fanny is noted as a good player (five handicap, began playing at age seven) who could give input on Faldo's very technical swing mechanics. She would regularly listen in on the range as instructor David Leadbetter gave Faldo some swing thoughts for the day. She was also famous for being a tireless worker, spending multiple hours walking a course before a tournament began.

"Fanny goes too far even for me," Faldo said. "We don't need to know every blade of grass out there. She'll spend six hours walking the course and getting yardages. But she has to do it that way. She finds it very difficult to do it any other way."

She also offered the camaraderie that was so instinctive in the Augusta National caddies.

"She's a rattler," Faldo said. "We were walking up the fourteenth hole at St. Andrews (on the Sunday of the 1990 British Open). I was leading by three or four when she turns to me and says, 'So, are you going to get a dog?' I knew what she was doing. She was trying to get me to switch off. It was a great little pressure relief."

Fanny worked with Faldo for four of his six major victories, missing only his 1987 British Open and 1989 Masters titles. She worked with Faldo for ten years until leaving in late 1999 to caddie briefly for Sergio Garcia before the temperamental Spaniard axed her before the 2000 Masters. By 2001 the Faldo-Fanny duet was back together.

Their close relationship was so in tune that they were each married on the same day (July 27, 2001) in separate cities.

First White Caddie

When Jack Tosone checked in at Masters Tournament headquarters on the Saturday before the 1983 Masters, he became the answer to a trivia question.

Tosone caddied for amateur Jim Hallet, a Bryant College (Midfield, Rhode Island) golf teammate, and became the first non–Augusta National caddie and first white caddie in Masters history. He just beat Tommy O'Toole, the caddie for amateur Jim Holtgrieve, to the punch.

The first day for Tosone was akin to being the nerdy freshman on the initial day at the new high school. He and Hallet were twenty-three-year-old college students in the company of older professionals, both players and caddies. After checking in at registration, Tosone went to the pro shop and was directed to see caddie master Freddie Bennett about acquiring the standard caddie jumpsuit. Bennett refused to give him one, saying that non–Augusta National caddies could not start until Sunday. When Tosone showed Bennett the rules he had received in the mail, Bennett promptly sent Tosone to the caddie shack.

He also got a chilly reception when he reached the facility.

"I walked in and there were about fifty or sixty guys, all playing cards or just sitting around," Tosone recalls today. "It was a smoky room, they all looked around at me and there was dead silence. All the guys were black. I just thought to myself, 'Oh, shit!' It was like a scene from some movie and I was the guy in the middle."

Finally, he pleaded his case and got the caddie supplies he needed.

"I think it was more of an economic thing than racial," Tosone says. "I emphasized to them I was amateur Jim Hallet's caddie, not the caddie of a pro golfer."

Since he checked in first, Tosone was assigned caddie locker No. 1. None other than Willie Peterson, the five-time Masters winner on Jack Nicklaus' bag, usually got that position and was not too happy about the outsider's new spot.

"He came up and said he wanted locker No. 1," Tosone says. "He was really the only one who gave me any trouble."

Peterson denied what occurred, but it was true to form for one of Augusta National's most outspoken caddies.

Hallet said he even heard from Peterson about the situation.

"Willie got up in my face and said, 'How dare your caddie take my locker,' " Hallet recalls today. "I couldn't believe a caddie was doing that to a player."

Hallet says that he hired Tosone because of their successful relationship in previous tournaments. Tosone was on his bag when Hallet reached the semifinals of the 1982 U.S. Amateur and earned a spot in the Masters field. Plus, Hallet admits he did not know much about Masters tradition.

"I was more of a hockey player," Hallet says. "I didn't know too much about Augusta at that time. I probably knew more about (Boston Bruins hockey great) Bobby Orr than I did about Bobby Jones."

Tosone knew more about the caddying business. He began caddying in New England as a sixth grader and told Jim that it would not be possible for him to work the Masters because he was not an Augusta National employee.

"I'm not black," Tosone remembers telling Hallet.

"We'll get you there somehow," Hallet came back. "I'll write a letter."

By the fall of 1982, Hallet learned of Augusta National Chairman Hord Hardin's change in policy for caddie hiring. He ran down the hall of his Bryant College dormitory, with an Augusta National press release in hand, to inform Tosone of the news.

"I'm there," Tosone quickly said.

Tosone's reception warmed up greatly when tournament play began at the 1983 Masters. Hallet, making his only career Masters appearance, was one stroke off the lead after a first-round 68. Through twenty-eight holes, he held the lead at 5-under par. Walking down the eleventh fairway in the second round, Tosone pointed to the leader board to the left of the green and noted the HALLET at the top. Playing with Arnold Palmer and Seve Ballesteros, he kept his cool until the par-3 sixteenth. His 8-iron tee shot landed inches from the right-front hole placement, but spun back quickly, down to the lower tier and into the pond. Hallet wound up with a double bogey and fell out of the lead.

He would go on to finish in a tie for fortieth at 9-over-par 297 and earned Low Amateur honors. Hallet turned pro soon after and played on the PGA Tour through the mid-1990s.

"When I walked in (after the first round), they were all shaking my hand, saying I did a good job," Tosone said. "I got more of that after the second round. The caddies there give you credit for doing a good job. I guess they realized I wasn't taking money out of their pockets. It was a great experience."

Tosone says the most difficult thing he found about the Augusta National course was reading the greens. Matthew "Shorty Mac" Palmer, Billy Casper's caddie, even helped him on some of the specifics during a practice round.

The 1983 Masters remains Tosone's only trip to Augusta. He now serves as the head professional at North Adams Country Club in Manchester, Vermont, and coaches the golf team at Massachusetts College of Liberal Arts. He still has some Masters trinkets, including two coveted Masters caddie hats, one with the cursive Caddie name and the other with a Masters logo.

"Some guy called me right after that tournament and said they were going to put my name in 'Trivial Pursuit,' " Tosone says of the game, which made its official introduction in 1982.

"I don't know if it ever happened. But it was supposed to say, 'Who broke the last color barrier in professional sports?' I'd love to have that card if it happened."

Today: Two Signs of the Times

The significance of Augusta National caddies in the Masters Tournament has clearly diminished over the past two decades. The caddie shack is not the same bustling center of activity that it used to be during the first full week in April. The banter at the Sand Hill Grill is usually reserved for other sports and activities instead of who is caddying for whom in the Masters. The men on the bag for Masters contenders now hail from places like Canada and New Zealand. There is little knowledge of the band of men who made the jumpsuits famous.

It is left to displays at Augusta National remembering the contribution of the caddies, such as what occurred in 2003, the twentieth anniversary of allowing outside caddies to work in the Masters. In the Exhibit Area on the left of the entrance corridor from the main gate during Masters Week, a mannequin fitted with a caddie jumpsuit and topped with a green caddie cap was presented. Behind glass was a golfer's bag, weighing approximately fifty pounds, for viewers to lift. A short story explaining the history of the caddies and their duties and mentioning Stovepipe, Cemetery, Iron Man, and Pappy was adjacent to the bag. The caddie display was so popular that it was scheduled to be shown again in 2004, in close proximity to the annual displays of trophies and crystal that Masters participants can win and tournament anniversary remembrances.

But every once in a while, there is still an actual glimpse back to the emotions and thrills that caddying in the Masters used to bring to these men who grew up with a tournament that has been Augusta's calling card for nearly three-quarters of a century.

Such a moment took place in 2002. A group of four caddies with Augusta National ties looped in that tournament. Jackson worked with Crenshaw for the twenty-sixth time, record longevity for a Masters caddie (it will reach twenty-eight years in 2004). Buck Moore, a former Augusta National caddie who has worked the PGA Tour for a variety of players, got a last-minute bag when Paul Azinger's regular Tour caddie, Terry Holt, could not reach Augusta because of the birth of a child the previous weekend. Jesse "Gray" Moore was on the bag of U.S. Mid-Amateur champion Tim Jackson. Louis Laurence was hired by Tommy Aaron to carry a Masters bag for the first time.

Jackson and Buck Moore are from the old school, black men who learned to caddie out of necessity, first at neighboring Augusta Country Club as preteens and then as they "graduated" to Augusta National, tutored by Stokes and Nipper. They caddied because it was a resource for money, first on the weekends and then full time. They made associations with the game's best players and eventually decided to make a living on the road caddying for a variety of journeymen or promising young players on various Tours.

Laurence and "Gray" Moore are white, a noteworthy description since the first white caddie did not pick up a bag in the Masters until 1983. Both men are Augusta natives who grew up in the shadow of the Masters during the 1960s, watching Arnold Palmer, Gary Player and Jack Nicklaus dominate. They were not brought up in the game as caddies, but instead played the game in hopes of following in the footsteps of "The Big Three."

They learned golf at two local municipal courses. The Augusta Golf Course is better known as "The Cabbage Patch" for its simple layout that skirts around the edge of Daniel Field, the small, private airport only a few miles from Augusta National. Historic Forest Hills Golf Club, a Donald Ross design, was the site of Bobby Jones' thirteen-stroke victory in the 1930

Southeastern Open, his final tournament start before he went on his Grand Slam run. At these courses, they mixed with Augusta's finest players, many of them black men, including current Champions Tour player Jim Dent, himself a former caddie at Augusta National. Often, they played high-stakes gambling matches.

Two of these men, Buck Moore and Laurence, had particularly prudent stories to tell as the 2002 golf season rolled from the West Coast to Florida and up toward Augusta. They were the past and the present.

For Buck, all eyes were on his chance to restore some of the lost glory of the Augusta National caddies.

Charles Howell III, the hotshot twenty-two-year-old Augusta native, was coming off a Rookie of the Year season on the PGA Tour in 2001. Charles, the son of an Augusta pediatric surgeon, was a self-proclaimed golf geek growing up next door to the Masters. One year, Ernie Els and Tom Watson were neighbors in rental homes during Masters Week, with Charles sharing a casual shoot around of driveway hoops with Watson. Charles first played Augusta National as a twelve-year-old, shooting 79. He learned the game at Augusta Country Club, the course that neighbors Amen Corner, and regularly visited swing guru David Leadbetter in Florida during his teen years to hone his game.

Howell's proximity to both Augusta National and the neighborhood of many of the caddies is particularly striking. To reach Howell's neighborhood and high school, Westminster School, travel from Augusta National up Berckmans Road, the bordering road just off the fifth fairway that is named after the Berckmans family, the owners of Fruitland Nurseries before Jones and Roberts discovered the land. A couple miles away, at the top of the hill, hang a right on Wheeler Road, an intersection that begins with Surrey Center, an assortment of upscale shops, offices and restaurants on the right corner, and a huge cemetery, Westover Memorial Park, on the left. Within blocks of this intersection is a black section, the Sand Hill, of modest homes where many caddies grew up. Eventually, Wheeler transitions into a prominent white residential area where Howell grew up, and the home of Westminster, a private school.

With a qualification for his first Masters all but in hand as 2001 wound down, Charles quietly pledged to make it a real Augusta affair, paying homage to the Augusta National caddies by hiring one of their own for the Masters. Picture this first-time scenario: A son of Augusta winning the Masters with another type of son of Augusta on his bag.

Charles was still searching for a regular caddie on the PGA Tour after Tony Navarro opted to remain with longtime boss Greg Norman early in 2002. In a small town like Augusta, everybody knew Charles' potential, particularly the caddies at Augusta National. Charles liked their association with his backyard tournament and their local knowledge, plus he had grown familiar enough to call them by their first names over the years by playing casual rounds at Forest Hills or Jones Creek Golf Club in neighboring Columbia County. In turn, the caddies favored Charles because of his bubbly personality and respectful nature; he more often than not ended sentences with a "Sir" or "Ma'am" when he first joined the Tour. He did not act like the spoiled rich kid that he could have become. Most folks just remembered him as "Little Charlie," a slight, bespectacled kid who had a knack for golf.

The tryouts for Howell's bag actually began the year before when Tommy "Burnt Biscuits" Bennett worked for Howell during the tail end of the 2001 season. Bennett had been Tiger Woods' first Masters caddie when Tiger made his amateur debut in 1995 and had bounced around various players on numerous Tours since leaving as an Augusta National regular.

That relationship was very short. Howell claimed that Bennett showed up for work all too often with beer on his breath. Then came the morning at the Las Vegas Invitational late in the fall when Tommy began the morning's conversation on the first tee with an under-his-breath request to borrow $500 and pay back a gambling debt from too long a night in the Vegas casinos. Bennett says the lure of the casinos is a problem all Tour caddies have in Vegas.

"Charles needed some chemistry, and they didn't have it,"

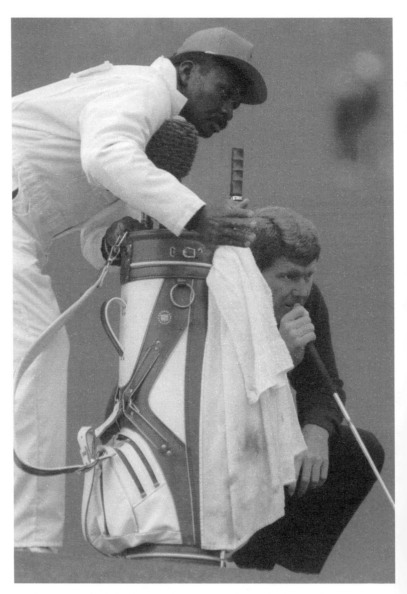

Buck Moore *(left)* helps Andy Bean read a putt during the Masters in the early 1990s. Moore, an Augusta native, grew up caddying at Augusta National and in the Masters and has worked on the PGA Tour for years. Moore almost caddied for Augustan Charles Howell III in the 2002 Masters. (© *Augusta Chronicle*)

said Dr. Charles Howell Jr., Charles' father who also serves as a close follower and confidant for his older son's career, along with mega-agency International Management Group.

Joe Collins was considered next, but "Joe has a raspy voice and it didn't work out. They couldn't find an understanding," Dr. Howell said. Joe never worked a tournament with Charles.

The Howells thought about talking with Jackson, but Carl's long and close association with Crenshaw prevented them from even making a serious inquiry.

"The first time I met him in person was at the New Orleans tournament in (the spring of) 2001," Jackson recalls of Howell. "I was caddying for Brad Fabel. And Charles just looked at me one day on the range, introduced himself, smiled and said, matter of factly, 'You and I are going to win the Masters one day.' I said let's do it. But nothing ever came of it."

Then came Buck Moore. A husky man with gray around the temples at age fifty-five, Buck once hoped to make it professionally as a pitcher in baseball, but injured his shoulder playing high school football at Augusta's oldest black high school, Lucy Laney. Buck is laid-back, speaks in a Southern baritone, and once supported his family by doubling as a truck driver and caddie. He began caddying at age twelve at Augusta National in 1966 and has worked in nearly thirty Masters, with a best finish of sixth with Ed Fiori in 1980. On the advice of the late LeRoy Schultz, Tom Weiskopf's former Masters caddie, Moore left Augusta National in 1988 to caddie for an assortment of players on the PGA Tour, including Kelly Gibson, K.J. Choi, Grant Waite, Fiori, and many others on a weekly basis. He still has not recorded a win, with a best finish of second.

"You can't get rich being a caddie," Moore says, "but you can live comfortably if your player does all right. I'd rather hit the lottery, though. I ain't got to have that much. I ain't greedy."

Buck pokes out his chest proudly for the well-known accomplishments of two of his children. Older son Otis played defensive tackle at Clemson University in the 1980s and was an All–Atlantic Coast Conference selection in 1989. After bouncing around a few NFL teams in the early 1990s, Otis was completing his playing career in the Arena Football League, playing the 2002 season as a six-feet-four, 270-pound, thirty-five-year-old two-way lineman for the New Jersey Gladiators. Younger son Ricky was the starting point guard and inspirational captain on the University of Connecticut's 1999 NCAA basketball championship team. Buck took a week off Gibson's bag to accompany wife Dorothy to the Final Four in St. Petersburg, Florida, that year, where University of Connecticut beat Duke, which also had an Augusta presence, William Avery, the great nephew of Iron Man Avery. Ricky, who at one time attended the same elementary school as Howell, is trying his wares in Europe in hopes of one day making an

Ricky Moore *(left)* and William Avery were honored in 1999 with the naming of the outdoor basketball court at Big Oak Park in the neighborhood where they grew up. Moore led the University of Connecticut to the 1999 NCAA men's basketball championship with a victory over Duke, which included Avery as a starting guard. Moore is the son of Buck Moore, a former Augusta National caddie, and Avery is the great nephew of Nathaniel "Iron Man" Avery, Arnold Palmer's caddie for his four Masters victories. (© *Augusta Chronicle*)

NBA roster. Even more proudly, Buck notes that Ricky earned a degree in four years at the Storrs, Connecticut, school.

"I know all those guys," Howell said of the Augusta National caddies at The Players Championship in March, one month before the 2002 Masters. "They keep urging me to hire one of them. If I do, I'll have all of them in my court. If I don't ...."

Howell prepped for the run toward Augusta by hiring Buck at the Phoenix Open in February. He called to inquire about Buck's availability a few weeks before.

"What are you doing now?" Charles asked.

"Starving," Buck replied.

"Come work for me, and you won't be starving any more," Howell said.

Charles earned $24,933 at Phoenix. At the Nissan Open two weeks later, Charles finished tied for sixth and carried home $123,950. The first stop on the Florida Swing came next and Charles won $10,798 at Doral, but shot 73-75 on the weekend. Total payout: Approximately $160,000, with Buck earning at least $16,000 with the normal ten percent caddie cut.

In the middle of this stretch, Howell became disgusted with his short game, particularly his putting, and felt a twinge of uncertainty about his working relationship with his caddie. Buck was not thought to be the necessary wise voice who would spur on a young player in a tight situation or provide the needed motivation when uncertainty struck, even though Buck admitted later, unsolicited, at the Masters that "Charles is the kind of player who needs talking to, a player where you've got to get in his head and tell him he's good, keep telling him that." Charles also insisted from the outset, in his own kind way, that Buck not spill the beans about a possible Masters job just yet. This was still just a trial. The next week, one of the golf weekly magazines carried a small news item where Moore was quoted not only talking about working the Masters but also possibly getting Howell's bag for the rest of the year.

"I have a hard enough time sticking my foot in my own mouth," says Howell, who had quickly become a media favorite for his candid interviews. "I didn't need two feet in my mouth."

Before the second stop in Florida, on the Monday of the Honda Classic, Buck received a phone call from Dr. Howell. It was five weeks before the Masters.

"I thought everything was going just fine," Buck says. "Then the phone rang and Charles' father just said, 'Charles and I think we need a change.' I asked him why Charles hadn't told me himself. He just said they had been thinking about making that decision for a couple of weeks."

Rumor was that Buck was hot about being laid off. He said he had only a passing "hello-hello" exchange with Charles since the parting. But come Masters time, Buck had evidently had a chance to cool down.

"No bad feelings," Buck says. "I wish (Charles) all the best. Ninety percent of the people here in Augusta were pulling for me to caddie for him. But it just didn't work out."

Perhaps Buck's anger lessened because he got a bag on Monday of Masters Week when Azinger was looking for a practice-round replacement for his sidelined caddie. Buck, on the grounds just as a spectator, was hanging around the clubhouse area, in the right place at the right time. When Azinger told his regular caddie to stay home with the newborn, Buck worked the tournament, even though Azinger missed the cut by one stroke.

"I just guess the good Lord does some mysterious things," Buck says.

Howell hired Bobby Conlan, a career caddie based at Pebble Beach Golf Links and Cypress Point Golf Club who had previously worked on Tour for Bobby Clampett, David Edwards, Clarence Rose, and won on Dave Eichelberger's bag at the 1999 U.S. Senior Open. Howell met Conlan on the Monterey Peninsula and used him on the bag at February's AT&T Pebble Beach National Pro-Am, where he finished twelfth earlier in the year, and then rehired him for the Bay Hill Invitational and The Players Championship before his first Masters appearance. Conlan's love for and knowledge of the course architecture of Dr. Alister Mackenzie, the designer of Cypress Point and Augusta National, was a main selling point.

Howell's first-round Masters debut was highlighted by his

clothing. The Swedish fashion designer Johan Lindeberg had put Charles in some offbeat golf clothing during most of the season, but for the Masters' first round, Charles sported white pants, flared at the bottom, with a forest green stripe down the sides. It looked like either the prison clothes Paul Newman wore in "Cool Hand Luke" or, more appropriately, the pants that Augusta National caddies sported in the old days of the jumpsuit.

Howell made the Masters cut by one stroke and finished tied for twenty-ninth at 3-over-par 291.

"I don't think Charles has found his full-time caddie yet," Dr. Howell said as the muddy weekend progressed at Augusta National.

By late summer, Howell had changed caddies again, hiring Brendan McCartain, who worked for José Maria Olazabal in his 1999 Masters victory. McCartain worked the 2002 Masters with Argentina's José Coceres, who was paired with Howell for the first two rounds. Howell said he and McCartain developed a friendship and mutual respect during those rounds. In the fall, McCartain was a key component when Howell captured his first PGA Tour title at the Michelob Championship at Kingsmill in Williamsburg, Virginia.

McCartain's proactive attitude may have brought on the victory. He was used to watching Olazabal's outstanding short game and was insistent on improving Howell's. He watched as Howell devoted more time to his game around the green. He helped Howell choose a new putter. Two weeks before the Michelob victory, McCartain grabbed Howell's 60-degree lob wedge out of his bag and took it to the Callaway Golf trailer on site at a tournament and had most of the bounce shaved off the bottom of the club. "Trust me, this will work," McCartain said. Howell went on to finish second in putting for the week.

"I spent a lot of time talking to Brendan about absolutely nothing," Howell said of his first victory. "We had conversation about some of the stupidest things, and he kept it going, which was the best thing ever. You know, Brendan won the '99 Masters with José Maria Olazabal, and I felt that anyone who can win that golf tournament has something to him, has some serious guts, and it showed today. He never blinked, his expression never changed. Where I was nervous as a cat on a hot tin roof at times, Brendan stayed the same and I wouldn't have known if I was in first or last place."

On the other hand, Louis Laurence would take just about any job just to get a place on the grounds at Augusta National.

The fifty-four-year old was a hotshot junior golfer in the mid-to-late 1960s. Many claim he was among the best junior golfers to come out of the Garden City, pre-Howell. He won the Augusta Junior, the city's most prestigious junior tournament, in 1965 and 1966 as a fifteen- and sixteen-year old. In other state and region tournaments, he was always among the best players in the field and led Richmond Academy's high school team to a state Class AAA title.

"From the time I was eight years old till I was fourteen, I played every day," Laurence says. "In the summer, my father would drop me off at 'The Patch' at 7:30 in the morning and I'd play eighteen holes in the morning, mess around and then play eighteen in the afternoon. I remember my mother and some of the other mothers would shine the headlights of their cars on the eighteenth green just so we could finish the last round."

Many compared his mannerisms to those of Palmer, his hero, and Laurence took that to heart. Laurence grimaced, slashed at the golf ball, putted knock-kneed on many occasions, and hitched up his pants just like Arnie. As an early teen, Laurence was known as a club thrower, until his father saw him break a club and threatened to take his clubs if Louis did not get rid of that temper, much as "Deacon" Palmer lectured a young Arnie on proper golf etiquette during the 1940s in Pennsylvania. Laurence even chose to attend Wake Forest, Arnie's alma mater, without a scholarship in the late 1960s at about the same time as Joe Inman and Leonard Thompson, future professional stars, were getting started at the Winston-Salem, North Carolina, school. After one year, Laurence dropped out, disillusioned about his game and college.

"It was like the world was coming to an end if I missed a

putt," Laurence said in an early 1970s interview with the *Augusta Chronicle*. "I guess people just didn't expect me to miss."

He resurfaced in the Navy in 1968, first stationed in Norfolk, Virginia, and then in Honolulu. He was the Navy's best golfer, earning all-Navy three times. His duty on an in-base submarine in Norfolk helped him "learn how to hit it straight." In Hawaii, the workload was more rigid, but he jumped around the Hawaiian Islands as a successful amateur and played in his only PGA Tour event, the 1971 Hawaiian Open, where he shot 77-80 to miss the cut.

Through all this time, Augusta still beckoned. His first wife, the former Gail Evans of Augusta, had delivered a son, Louis Jr. Augusta College, now Augusta State University, soon offered a full ride for golf, which the 23-year-old Laurence accepted following his four-year Navy stint. For three years, Laurence played the No. 1 or No. 2 position for the Jaguars, whose home course was Forest Hills.

That is about as far as his competitive game reached. He worked in various jobs outside of the game until becoming an assistant golf professional at Forest Hills in 1979. He was an assistant at Goshen Plantation Country Club and gave lessons at a driving range in North Augusta, South Carolina. In the meantime, he got a divorce and his son died in a 1999 automobile accident in Massachusetts.

Over twenty years later, the lure of Augusta National finally got him.

He took the unusual turn of becoming a caddie at Augusta National in his early forties in the late 1980s. Freddie Bennett, a good friend, convinced him to try caddying at Augusta National.

"You ought to try it as much as you know about golf and love it," said Bennett, who lives near Laurence today.

"I didn't know Augusta National was taking on caddies," Laurence said.

"Sure, we've got lots of white boys out there," Bennett said with a laugh.

By January 1989, Laurence was hooked. His first bag at Augusta National was Donny Anderson, the former Green

Louis Laurence *(left)* helps Tommy Aaron, the 1973 Masters champion, pick a club during the 2002 Masters. Laurence grew up in Augusta and was a promising junior player in the 1960s. Aaron hired Laurence in 2002 and 2003, possibly his last two Masters appearances as a participant. (© *Augusta Chronicle*)

Bay Packers halfback. He would later tote for former Miami Dolphins coach Don Shula and Atlanta Braves pitcher John Smoltz and carried in the same group as pop singer Celine Dion and her husband. He has a picture with Celine as they stood on the tee of the par-3 twelfth hole. Two years ago, when he was laid off his full-time job at Augusta's Thermal Ceramics for a second time, he asked Van Dorn if a summer job was available elsewhere to make caddying his year-round occupation.

He now caddies at Augusta National from the club's opening in early October until it closes for the summer in late May. For the last three years, he has then trekked to Kohler, Wisconsin, in the summer to caddie at another Caddie Master Enterprises course, Whistling Straits Golf Club, a top-flight club that will play host to the 2004 PGA Championship. That tradition of traveling from Augusta National in the off-season dated back to the 1960s. A large group of Augusta National caddies would spend the summer in Atlantic City, New Jersey, as everything from caddies to cooks to bellhops. Laurence arrives at Whistling Straits at sunrise during the long Wisconsin summers and carries twice a day for as many days as possible. Laurence also remarried, in 1998 to Judith, a woman he had met twenty years before when he helped tutor her son in golf at Forest Hills.

"Being away from her is tough," Laurence says. "But she understands this is what I do and love. Plus, she doesn't mind the checks coming back in the mail."

Two months before the 2002 Masters, Laurence's connection with his childhood dream course became even more of a reality. He was picked to caddie for Aaron, who came into town to check out the massive changes made to the course since 2001.

Aaron had picked an Augusta National caddie for the last few years, using Joe Collins in 2000 and even allowing *Sports Illustrated* writer Rick Reilly to step in for Augusta National regular Freddie Robertson for one round in 2001 as Reilly researched a book on various caddie duties.

"I used my Tour caddie until the last few years," Aaron

said in 2000, when, at age sixty-three, he became the oldest player in Masters history to make the cut. "But it's so hard for my regular guy to find accommodations. He lives in Arizona and would have had to come all the way back here to caddie. So I just decided to use a local caddie."

Aaron's magical 2000 Masters included a first-round, even-par 72 that was one of only twelve rounds of par or better and three better than Tiger Woods' first-round 75. Aaron followed with a 74 to make the cut, then tired on the weekend with 86-81 for a 313 total, last in the field of weekend finishers, but good enough to earn $10,488. Aaron was one of the few players in the field who had experience with an Augusta National caddie, using Cleveland Randolph on the way to a victory in the 1973 Masters.

"Joe is all I know," Aaron said of Collins in 2000 when asked about his Augusta National caddie. "He didn't hit a bad shot or a bad putt all week. I asked Joe for some advice on a putt on the first hole, just to get his opinion, just to see what he'd have to say. But I read most all my putts and clubbed myself."

Aaron, a Gainesville, Georgia, native, was among the dying breed of aging Masters winners still willing to walk the steep hills of Augusta National and possibly embarrass themselves by shooting rounds in the 80s. Aaron had rarely played on the Champions Tour over the past few years, but coming to Augusta reminded him of his youth and his most brilliant golf moment. A caddie who gets Aaron's bag, and some others such as Seve Ballesteros, Charles Coody, Billy Casper, Gay Brewer, or Doug Ford, was virtually assured—barring a great start like Aaron in 2000—of watching golf from behind the ropes on the weekend and making a lesser payday.

But that did not matter to Laurence. He and Aaron hit it off quickly during the February practice round, and Aaron asked if Laurence would be available to caddie in the Masters.

The request shocked Laurence. He quickly accepted the offer and wrote his name and address on a scorecard for Aaron's reference.

As the Masters moved closer, no follow-up came from

Aaron. Laurence figured that the 1973 Masters champion's plans had changed. So Laurence opted to spend the week as a lowly forecaddie at Augusta Country Club, a job where he would search for errant drives instead of toting a bag. His only view of the Masters would be over the fence that separates Augusta Country Club's ninth fairway from Amen Corner.

However, two days before Masters Week, as Laurence completed caddie duty for an Augusta National member, he was approached by Dale Fryer, the head of outside services for Augusta National. Aaron had finally called to make his final request for Laurence to work during the Masters.

"I lived my whole life to get here," Laurence said. "Actually, to play here. But I'm not going to make it playing. So this is a dream come true for me."

Laurence caddied in practice-round groups that included Phil Mickelson, Mark Calcavecchia, Fred Couples, and Jim Furyk. Aaron and Coody, the 1971 Masters champion, were paired together for the first two rounds.

It did not matter that Aaron shot 79-78–157 to miss the cut. The experience was priceless. Whether it was the sixty-five-year-old Aaron acting like a nervous rookie on the first tee or carving a fairway wood into one of Augusta National's newly lengthened par 4s, Laurence was in heaven. On occasion, Laurence thought he saw an opportunity to offer a suggestion on club selection or the subtle break of a putt. Then he remembered this was not just a high-handicap member he was working with.

"It's intimidating to be in someone's presence who has won the Masters," Laurence said. "They have a confidence on the golf course that is just unnatural."

Laurence earned $700 for his five-day stint with Aaron. The relationship went so smoothly that when Aaron returned in 2003, Laurence was back on the bag. The sixty-six-year-old Aaron sloshed around soggy Augusta National, beginning the tournament bogey, triple bogey, double bogey on the way to a front-nine 47 and a 92-80 thirty-six holes, the highest halfway total in the tournament.

Laurence may also have been the final caddie of Aaron's

Masters career. In 2002, Augusta National Chairman Hootie Johnson announced that past champions would have to meet minimum playing requirements during the year to participate after age sixty-five, precluding their previous lifetime invitation. However, the week before the 2003 Masters, Nicklaus and Palmer met with Johnson and the policy was rescinded to "play as long as they like, so long as they feel they remain competitive."

"He can still play," Laurence said of Aaron after the second round was completed in 2002. "When the gallery claps for him, like they did when he finished his round today, it sends chills up your spine. When he manufactures a shot into these greens with a fairway wood or long iron, you realize that this man has some kind of game. You forget it sometimes, but these guys were the best at one time."

The same holds true for the famed Augusta National caddies.

Masters Champions and Caddies

Year	Champion	Caddie	Number
1934	Horton Smith	NA	NA
1935	Gene Sarazen	Thor "Stovepipe" Nordwall	NA
1936	Horton Smith	NA	NA
1937	Byron Nelson	Fred Searles	NA
1938	Henry Picard	Willie "Pappy" Stokes	NA
1939	Ralph Guldahl	NA	NA
1940	Jimmy Demaret	Banny Smalley	NA
1941	Craig Wood	Pearly Dawsey	30
1942	Byron Nelson	Fred Searles	12
1946	Herman Keiser	Thomas Evans	41
1947	Jimmy Demaret	Banny Smalley	69
1948	Claude Harmon	Willie "Pappy" Stokes	12
1949	Sam Snead	O'Bryant Williams	35
1950	Jimmy Demaret	Banny Smalley	37
1951	Ben Hogan	Willie "Pappy" Stokes	6
1952	Sam Snead	O'Bryant Williams	42
1953	Ben Hogan	Willie "Pappy" Stokes	2
1954	Sam Snead	O'Bryant Williams	62
1955	Cary Middlecoff	Clarence "Eight-Ball" Harris	7
1956	Jack Burke Jr.	Willie "Pappy" Stokes	8
1957	Doug Ford	George "Fireball" Franklin	57
1958	Arnold Palmer	Nathaniel "Iron Man" Avery	85
1959	Art Wall Jr.	Henry Hammond	83
1960	Arnold Palmer	Nathaniel "Iron Man" Avery	13
1961	Gary Player	Ernest "Snipes" Nipper	52
1962	Arnold Palmer	Nathaniel "Iron Man" Avery	13
1963	Jack Nicklaus	Willie Peterson	49
1964	Arnold Palmer	Nathaniel "Iron Man" Avery	82
1965	Jack Nicklaus	Willie Peterson	90
1966	Jack Nicklaus	Willie Peterson	90
1967	Gay Brewer	Johnny Frank Moore	6
1968	Bob Goalby	Frank "Marble Eye" Stokes	21
1969	George Archer	Frank "Skinny" Ware	63
1970	Billy Casper	Matthew "Shorty Mac" Palmer	34
1971	Charles Coody	Walter "Cricket" Pritchett	7

Year	Champion	Caddie	Number
1972	Jack Nicklaus	Willie Peterson	16
1973	Tommy Aaron	Cleveland Randolph	68
1974	Gary Player	Eddie "E.B." McCoy	39
1975	Jack Nicklaus	Willie Peterson	76
1976	Raymond Floyd	Fred "Hop" Harrison	36
1977	Tom Watson	Leon McCladdie	26
1978	Gary Player	Eddie "E.B." McCoy	52
1979	Fuzzy Zoeller	Jariah Beard	48
1980	Seve Ballesteros	Marion Herrington	10
1981	Tom Watson	Leon McCladdie	32
1982	Craig Stadler	Ben Bussey	41
1983	Seve Ballesteros	Nicholas DePaul	6
1984	Ben Crenshaw	Carl Jackson	52
1985	Bernhard Langer	Peter Coleman	9
1986	Jack Nicklaus	Jack Nicklaus II	89
1987	Larry Mize	Scott Steele	72
1988	Sandy Lyle	David Musgrove	63
1989	Nick Faldo	Andy Prodger	36
1990	Nick Faldo	Fanny Sunesson	1
1991	Ian Woosnam	Phillip Morby	9
1992	Fred Couples	Joe LaCava	70
1993	Bernhard Langer	Peter Coleman	11
1994	José Maria Olazabal	Dave Renwick	54
1995	Ben Crenshaw	Carl Jackson	16
1996	Nick Faldo	Fanny Sunesson	67
1997	Tiger Woods	Mike "Fluff" Cowan	71
1998	Mark O'Meara	Jerry Higgenbothem	73
1999	José Maria Olazabal	Brendan McCartain	17
2000	Vijay Singh	Dave Renwick	19
2001	Tiger Woods	Steve Williams	71
2002	Tiger Woods	Steve Williams	1
2003	Mike Weir	Brennan Little	57

Bibliography

Augusta Chronicle, www.augustaarchives.com

Boston Globe. August 26, 1990.

Champions Tour Media Guide, 2003.

Christian, Frank. *Augusta National and the Masters.* Chelsea, Mich.: Sleeping Bear Press, 1996.

Crenshaw, Ben, with Melanie Hauser. *A Feel for the Game.* New York: Doubleday, 2001.

Golf Digest, April 1993.

Golf Digest, December 1998.

Golf Digest, May 2002.

Golf Digest, March 2001.

Green, Ron Sr. *Shouting at Amen Corner.* Charlotte, N.C.: Charlotte Observer, 1999.

Masters Journal, 1994.

Masters Media Guide, 2003.

Masters Tournament Player and Caddie List, 1984–2003.

Nicklaus, Jack, with Ken Bowden. *My Story.* New York: Simon & Schuster, 1997.

Owen, David. *The Making of the Masters.* New York: Simon & Schuster, 1999.

Palmer, Arnold, with James Dodson. *A Golfer's Life.* New York: Ballantine Publishing Group, 1999.

PGA Tour 2003, Official PGA Tour Media Guide

Price, Charles. *A Golf Story.* New York: Macmillan, 1986.

Sampson, Curt. *Hogan.* Nashville, Tenn.: Rutledge-Hill, 1996.

Sarazen, Gene. *Thirty Years of Championship Golf.* New York: Prentice-Hall, 1950.

Davis, Martin. *The Hogan Mystique.* Greenwich, Conn.: American Golfer, Inc., 1994.

Sports Illustrated, April 15, 1957.

Sports Illustrated, April 17, 1995.

Sports Illustrated, April 1, 1998.

Sports Illustrated, April 10, 2000.

Sports Illustrated, April 17, 2000.

Van Natta, Don Jr. *First Off the Tee.* New York: Public Affairs, 2003.